# The Uncomfortable Conversation

*Negotiation for People Who Hate Conflict*

Matthew Thomas

# Disclaimer

We're sharing strategies that work based on research and experience, but negotiation outcomes vary wildly depending on circumstances, industry, and organizational culture. Employment law differs by location, so check local regulations about salary history questions and workplace negotiations before trying anything here. The salary figures and projections are examples, not guarantees. We're not lawyers or financial advisors. Names and details in examples have been changed.

# Acknowledgments

Hundreds of people shared their negotiation stories over the years, the successes and the failures and the times they froze completely. Those conversations made it clear that standard advice doesn't help when we find the entire process terrifying.

The people who read early drafts and said "this part still sounds like generic career advice" made everything sharper. The ones who admitted they still wouldn't negotiate helped clarify we're not trying to convince anyone, just giving tools to people who could act if they had better infrastructure.

Writing about money required examining uncomfortable patterns in our own lives. The people who made space for that mess made the work possible.

What follows is for everyone who's accepted less because asking felt impossible, and for everyone who'll negotiate despite the terror because the alternative costs too much.

# The Conversation That Costs Half a Million Dollars

The conversation most people avoid costs them somewhere between $400,000 and $1,000,000 over a career, and the reason isn't complicated. Sitting across from someone who has power over our income and asking them for more money feels like standing naked while they decide whether we're worth it, and most of us would rather just take whatever number they offer than endure fifteen minutes of that particular flavor of terror.

We're not talking about people who lack information or people who don't understand how negotiation works in theory. We're talking about the ones who research salary ranges obsessively, who write scripts in the shower, who rehearse exact phrases while driving to the interview, and then when the hiring manager says "we're offering you $68,000," we hear ourselves say "that sounds great" before our brain even has time to process what just happened. The script we practiced for three days evaporates the second we need it because our body has decided this conversation is a threat to our survival and has shut down everything except the part that wants to make the discomfort stop immediately.

This pattern shows up in data that's almost boring in its consistency. About 60% of people who receive job offers don't negotiate at all, and when researchers ask why, the answers cluster around the same themes: fear the offer will get pulled entirely, fear of damaging the relationship before we even start, fear of looking greedy or difficult or ungrateful, fear of the particular kind of rejection that comes from someone telling us we're not worth what we think we're worth. The physical sensations that accompany these fears aren't subtle. Heart rate spikes, voice shakes, mind goes blank right when we need to be most articulate, and the urge to end the conversation and escape becomes so overwhelming that accepting whatever they offered feels like relief rather than resignation.

Most negotiation advice doesn't help us because it's written for people who find this kind of conversation merely uncomfortable rather than genuinely terrifying. We get told to "know our worth" and "advocate for ourselves" and "don't leave money on the table," which is accurate but completely useless when what we actually need is the exact sentence to say when our throat is closing up and our brain is screaming at us to just say yes and get out of there. The gap between understanding that we should negotiate and being able to actually do it isn't a knowledge problem, it's a nervous system problem, and treating it like we just need more confidence or better mindset is like telling someone having a panic attack to calm down and think positive thoughts.

The financial stakes are real enough that we can't just write this off as a personality quirk we'll work around. A $5,000 difference in starting salary at age 25 becomes $634,000 by age 65 when we account for standard raises and compound investment returns, and most of us have no concept that the numbers work this way because nobody explains it in terms that make the math feel urgent. We think we're choosing between $68,000 and $73,000, which sounds like the difference between having a slightly nicer apartment or not, but what we're actually choosing is whether to start a compounding process that will either build wealth over decades or leave us hundreds of thousands of dollars behind someone who's doing identical work but negotiated their first offer.

Women who negotiate consistently throughout their careers earn between $1,000,000 and $1,500,000 more than women who don't, not because of massive one-time wins but because negotiation works through accumulation. Each raise builds on the previous salary, each new job offer anchors to the last number, each bonus calculation uses base salary as the starting point, which means a single conversation where we accepted less than we should have doesn't just cost us that year's difference, it resets the baseline for every financial conversation we'll have for the next decade. The gap isn't visible in the moment because we're comparing ourselves to what we had before rather than to what we could have had, and by the time we realize how far behind we've fallen, we're 15 years into a career and the distance feels impossible to close.

The advice industry around negotiation tends to assume we're starting from a place of basic comfort with conflict, that what we need is technique refinement rather than permission to feel how we actually feel about this. We get frameworks and tactics and strategies that all presume we can walk into the room without our body staging a full revolt against what we're about to do. The unstated premise is that negotiation is a skill like any other, something we can learn through practice and improve through iteration, which is technically true but misses the part where most of us can't get to the practice phase because the fear stops us before we even try.

What actually helps conflict-averse people negotiate isn't motivation or inspiration or stories about how other people did it successfully. What helps is having the exact words to say, written out in advance, so when our brain goes blank we have something concrete to fall back on rather than improvising in the moment when we're least capable of thinking clearly. What helps is understanding why our body reacts the way it does to this specific conversation, not so the reaction goes away but so we can plan around it instead of being ambushed by it every time. What helps is knowing that most hiring managers expect negotiation and won't think less of us for asking, even though our anxiety insists they'll be offended and withdraw the offer, and having that information doesn't make the fear disappear but it does give us one small piece of ground to stand on when everything else feels unstable.

We're not trying to become different people or perform a version of confidence we don't actually feel. We're not aiming to walk into salary conversations with the ease of someone who finds conflict energizing rather than depleting. What we're doing is building a toolkit that works for people whose natural instinct is to avoid confrontation, who would genuinely rather leave money on the table than sit through awkwardness, who need this process to be as scripted and predictable as possible because spontaneity in high-stakes moments is where we fall apart.

The structure here is straightforward. We start with why this feels impossible, walking through the physiology of what happens in our body when we even think about negotiating and why understanding that response matters. Then we move into the actual dollar amounts at stake because we need to see the real numbers to make a clear decision about whether fifteen minutes of discomfort is worth hundreds of thousands of dollars over a career. From there we get into what was taught to us about money and asking for things, all the early programming that makes negotiation feel morally wrong rather than just scary, because those messages don't evaporate when we enter the workforce even though we wish they would.

The second part covers what actually works for people like us. Preparation that reduces panic by moving decisions out of the high-stress moment. Exact scripts for every common scenario, written to be copied word-for-word rather than adapted or personalized. Managing the physical response that shows up even when we're prepared, all the practical tactics for when our voice shakes or our mind goes blank or we want to bolt from the room. What to do when they say no and how to keep the conversation going instead of accepting the first refusal. The gender dynamics that make this harder for women in ways that aren't about individual behavior but about systemic bias in how identical actions get interpreted differently based on who's doing them.

The final section looks at building this as a skill without requiring us to fundamentally change who we are. Starting small with low-stakes practice where rejection won't cost us financially. What to do with the money after we negotiate for it, because many of us get the raise and then immediately spend it in ways that don't match why we asked for it in the first place. The reality that this isn't one conversation but a pattern we'll repeat for the next 30 or 40 years, and each instance stays uncomfortable but gets slightly more manageable when we have tools that actually work for conflict-averse people.

We're not promising this will become easy or that we'll ever enjoy it. We're saying the cost of avoiding it is too high to ignore, and there are specific concrete things we can do that make it possible to get through the conversation even when everything in us wants to run. The choice isn't between negotiating comfortably or not negotiating at all. The choice is between having the fifteen-minute conversation that makes us want to throw up or leaving somewhere between $400,000 and $1,000,000 on the table over the next few decades, and neither option feels good, but one of them costs significantly more than the other.

## The Body Decides Before the Brain Does

The email arrives at 2:47 p.m. on a Tuesday with the subject line "Offer Letter," and before we even open it, our heart rate changes. Not dramatically, not panic-attack-level elevation, just a small uptick that registers somewhere in our chest as we click through to see the number. The offer is $68,000, which is $7,000 less than what we researched, and the rational part of our brain knows we should respond with a counteroffer because we've literally spent two weeks preparing for this exact moment. We have a script saved in our notes app. We practiced saying the words out loud three times yesterday. And yet within 90 seconds of reading that email, we've already typed "Thank you so much, this is perfect, when do I start?" because the alternative felt physically unbearable.

What happened in those 90 seconds wasn't a conscious decision to accept less money than we're worth. What happened was a full-body threat response that hijacked every system designed to help us think clearly, and by the time our prefrontal cortex caught up with what was happening, we'd already hit send on an email that just cost us roughly $480,000 over the next 30 years. Understanding why our body does this doesn't make the response go away, but it does give us room to work around it instead of being completely at its mercy, and that difference matters when the financial stakes are this high.

The sequence starts in the amygdala, which is the part of our brain that processes threat before we're consciously aware anything is wrong. The amygdala doesn't distinguish between physical danger and social danger, which means the threat of someone thinking we're greedy or difficult registers the same way as the threat of someone attacking us in a parking lot. When it detects something it categorizes as dangerous, it triggers the hypothalamus, which activates the sympathetic nervous system, which dumps cortisol and adrenaline into our bloodstream, which is why our hands start sweating and our heart starts racing before we've even formed a thought about what we're going to say. This entire cascade happens in milliseconds, and we experience it as a sudden overwhelming urge to make the discomfort stop by whatever means necessary, which in salary negotiation usually means agreeing to whatever terms will end the conversation fastest.

Cortisol is helpful when we actually need to run from danger because it sharpens focus and increases physical readiness, but in a negotiation it does the opposite of what we need. High cortisol impairs working memory, makes it harder to access information we know we have, and narrows our thinking to immediate escape rather than strategic planning. This is why we can spend three days memorizing a negotiation script and then go completely blank the second we need it, not because we didn't prepare enough but because the stress response has temporarily locked us out of the parts of our brain where that information lives. We're sitting there trying to remember what we planned to say while our body is screaming that we're in danger and need to agree to whatever makes the danger stop.

The physical sensations show up differently for different people but they cluster around predictable patterns. Some of us get a tight feeling in our chest that makes it hard to breathe normally. Some get a sensation of heat rising into our face and neck. Some get shaky hands or a voice that won't stay steady. Some get nausea or a feeling like our stomach just dropped. Some get a kind of mental fog where we can hear the other person talking but can't quite process what they're saying in real time. What all of these have in common is that they make the conversation feel actively dangerous, not just uncomfortable, and our body's solution to danger is either fight or flight or freeze, none of which help us negotiate effectively.

Introverts experience this response more intensely than extroverts because of baseline differences in how our brains process stimulation and arousal. Extroverts have lower baseline arousal, which means they need more stimulation to feel engaged and alert, and conflict provides that stimulation in a way they find energizing rather than overwhelming. Introverts have higher baseline arousal, which means we're already operating closer to our threshold for overstimulation, and conflict pushes us past that threshold into a state where everything feels too loud and too much and we just want it to stop. This isn't about being shy or lacking social skills, it's about dopamine sensitivity and cortisol reactivity, actual neurological differences that make high-stakes conversations genuinely more physiologically taxing for us than for people with different wiring.

Dopamine is part of the reward system, and it's what makes extroverts feel good when they win arguments or push back in negotiations. Their brains release dopamine during conflict, which creates a positive feedback loop where engaging feels rewarding. Introverts don't get that dopamine hit from conflict, or we get a much smaller one, which means there's no natural reward to offset the cortisol spike. We're just getting the stress without the accompanying feeling of exhilaration, which is why negotiations drain us in a way they don't drain people who are wired differently. This explains why we can understand intellectually that negotiation is important and still find ourselves avoiding it at every opportunity, because our body is telling us the truth about how it experiences the process even if that truth costs us money.

The three specific fears that trigger the threat response are predictable enough that researchers have names for them, though the terminology doesn't matter as much as recognizing them when they show up. The first is fear of tangible loss: they'll rescind the offer entirely, we'll lose the job, we'll end up with nothing instead of less-than-we-wanted-but-still-something. This fear isn't completely irrational because offers do occasionally get pulled, though it happens far less often than our anxiety suggests, and the risk of losing an offer because we negotiated professionally is much lower than the cost of accepting every first offer for the next 30 years. The second fear is relationship damage: we'll start the job having already made our new boss think we're difficult or ungrateful, we'll be marked as a problem before we even begin, and every interaction afterward will carry the weight of that first negative impression. The third fear is emotional pain: they'll tell us no and we'll have to sit with the feeling of being told we're not worth what we think we're worth, which hits directly at our sense of self in ways that feel genuinely dangerous even though logically we know a salary negotiation isn't a referendum on our value as humans.

These fears aren't distinct categories that show up separately. They tangle together and amplify each other so that by the time we're actually in the negotiation, we're not thinking about salary bands and market rates, we're thinking about all the ways this could go catastrophically wrong and how much we want to avoid experiencing any of them. The hiring manager says "we're offering $68,000" and what we hear is "we think this is what you're worth and if you disagree you're ungrateful and we might take the offer away and you'll have ruined everything," which is obviously not what they said but that's what our amygdala is processing in the moment.

What this looks like in real time varies but the core pattern holds. We get the offer email and immediately feel our chest tighten. We open the document and see a number that's lower than expected and feel heat rise into our face. We start typing a response and our hands shake slightly. We write a sentence asking for more money and then delete it because even seeing those words on screen makes our heart race. We write something enthusiastic and accommodating instead and hit send before we can second-guess it, and then we feel relief for approximately 90 seconds before the realization hits that we just accepted $7,000 less than we should have and that number will follow us through every subsequent salary conversation for the next decade.

The voice shaking is particularly brutal because it's visible to the other person in a way that internal sensations aren't. We can have a racing heart and they won't know, but we can't hide vocal tremor, and the fear that they'll hear us sounding nervous makes the shaking worse in a feedback loop that's almost impossible to interrupt once it starts. This is the body's betrayal we can't control: we've decided we're going to negotiate, we've prepared what to say, and then our voice gives us away by sounding uncertain or scared even when we're saying words we fully mean. The temptation is to interpret this as a sign we shouldn't be negotiating at all, that our body knows something our conscious mind doesn't, but that's backward. The body is reacting to perceived social danger, not to actual inappropriateness of the request.

The urge to end the conversation immediately shows up as an almost physical pressure to just agree and get out of there. This isn't about logically deciding to accept their offer, it's about our nervous system calculating that the fastest way to reduce the stress is to eliminate the source of the stress, which is the conversation itself. We can feel this urge as a kind of claustrophobia, like the room is getting smaller and we need to escape, or as a sudden overwhelming fatigue where continuing the discussion feels too exhausting to contemplate. The relief we feel when we accept their first offer isn't about being happy with the salary, it's about the stress response finally powering down now that the threat has been eliminated by compliance.

Understanding the evolutionary logic here helps a little bit with the self-judgment that usually follows. Our ancestors who worried excessively about social rejection and status hierarchy were more likely to stay integrated in their groups, which meant better survival odds in environments where being cast out was often fatal. The people who didn't care what others thought of them might have been more comfortable asking for things, but they also might have gotten kicked out of the tribe and died alone, which meant their genes didn't get passed forward as reliably. We inherited nervous systems that are extremely sensitive to social threat because that sensitivity kept our ancestors alive, and the fact that it now costs us money in salary negotiations doesn't change the deep wiring that makes the response feel life-or-death even when we know it isn't.

This isn't an excuse for accepting low offers, it's context for why the advice to "just be confident" or "know your worth" doesn't land for us the way it apparently lands for people who find negotiation straightforward. We can know our worth in every objective sense and still have our body shut down the conversation because it's perceiving danger that we can't logic our way out of. The solution isn't to eliminate the fear response, which isn't possible without medication or years of exposure therapy, but to build systems that work with the response instead of requiring it to disappear before we can act.

What this looks like practically is having scripts prepared in advance so we're not trying to compose sentences while cortisol is destroying our working memory. Recording ourselves saying the script out loud multiple times so our voice has muscle memory to fall back on when our brain goes blank. Building in pauses where we don't talk at all, which gives our nervous system time to regulate instead of staying in escalating panic. Requesting time to think rather than responding in the moment when we're least capable of clear thought. These aren't dramatic interventions that transform how we feel about negotiation, they're small adjustments that make it possible to get through the conversation even when our body is staging a full revolt against what we're doing.

The body decides before the brain does, and we can't change that sequence, but we can decide what happens after the initial spike. We can recognize the physical sensations as a threat response rather than accurate information about danger. We can slow down instead of rushing to end the discomfort. We can use preparation to bypass the parts of our brain that stop working under stress. None of this makes negotiation comfortable, but it does make it possible, and possible is enough when the alternative is leaving hundreds of thousands of dollars on the table because our amygdala thinks asking for fair compensation is equivalent to facing down a predator.

The timeline of how this response unfolds matters because it helps us identify intervention points where we can interrupt the cascade before it fully takes over. The initial trigger happens the moment we see the offer number or the moment we sit down for a salary conversation with our manager, and within 200 milliseconds the amygdala has processed this as potential threat and started the physiological response. We're not consciously aware of anything yet except maybe a vague sense of unease, but our body is already preparing for danger. By the time we've consciously registered what's happening, maybe two or three seconds in, our heart rate has increased, our breathing has shifted, and cortisol is starting to circulate. At the five-second mark, we're feeling the full effects: tight chest, racing thoughts, strong urge to resolve the situation immediately.

Most of us make our critical mistakes in that five-to-thirty-second window, which is when the stress response is at its peak but we're still trying to engage with the conversation as if our brain is working normally. We hear "we're offering you $68,000" at second zero, we feel panic rising at second three, we open our mouth to respond at second eight, and what comes out is "that sounds great, thank you" because that's the fastest route to making the stress stop. The whole sequence from trigger to acceptance can happen in under fifteen seconds, and once we've said yes, walking it back feels nearly impossible even though objectively we could send a follow-up email saying we need to discuss the compensation further.

Understanding this timeline gives us one specific tool: building in mandatory pauses between receiving information and responding to it. If we know the danger zone is that first fifteen to thirty seconds, we can create a rule for ourselves that we never respond to a salary offer or raise discussion in real time. We always say some version of "let me take a day to think about the full package and I'll get back to you tomorrow," which moves the decision point out of the high-stress window into a time when our brain is functioning normally. This sounds simple enough that it barely counts as strategy, but in practice it's one of the most effective interventions for anxiety-driven acceptance of low offers because it eliminates the possibility of stress-based yes.

The challenge with implementing this pause is that it goes against every social instinct we have about polite responsiveness. When someone offers us something, the expected response is immediate gratitude and acceptance, and deviating from that script feels rude or difficult even though it's completely normal business practice. Hiring managers and bosses are used to people taking time to consider offers. They expect it. The awkwardness we're imagining about asking for time to think is almost entirely in our heads, a product of anxiety rather than reality, but it feels real enough that we override our own best interests to avoid it.

The voice shaking problem deserves its own examination because it's such a visible marker of our internal state and because it triggers a secondary shame response that makes everything worse. When our voice shakes, we immediately become self-conscious about the shaking, which increases our stress level, which makes the shaking worse, which makes us more self-conscious in a loop that's very hard to exit once it starts. The physiological mechanism is that stress tightens the muscles around our vocal cords, which affects our ability to control pitch and volume precisely, and this happens before we can consciously decide to steady our voice. By the time we notice we sound shaky, the muscles are already tense and there's no quick way to relax them through willpower alone.

What actually helps with vocal shaking is accepting that it's happening rather than trying to suppress it, which paradoxically reduces it because we stop adding the secondary stress of fighting the symptom. If our voice shakes during a negotiation, we can acknowledge it directly with something like "I get nervous in these conversations but I mean what I'm saying," which takes the power out of it by naming it rather than pretending it's not happening. Most people on the receiving end of a shaky-voiced negotiation aren't judging us for being nervous, they're just trying to understand what we're asking for, and the shakiness becomes much less relevant once we've acknowledged it and moved forward with the actual content.

The mind-going-blank problem is related but distinct from the voice issue because it's about access to information rather than physical control. We know what we want to say, we prepared exactly what we were going to say, and then in the moment we can't retrieve any of it because the stress has temporarily interfered with our working memory and retrieval processes. This isn't about intelligence or preparation quality, it's about cortisol doing what cortisol does under stress, which is prioritize immediate survival responses over complex cognitive functions like remembering carefully crafted arguments about market rates and value propositions.

The solution for blank-mind moments is having the script written down physically in front of us, not as a backup plan but as the primary plan. We're not trying to remember what we were going to say, we're reading what we wrote when we were capable of clear thought. This only works if we've actually written it down ahead of time in enough detail that we can read it verbatim without having to fill in gaps, and if we've given ourselves permission to reference notes during the conversation rather than treating that as some kind of failure. Lawyers read from notes during trials, executives read from scripts during earnings calls, politicians read from teleprompters during speeches, and somehow we've convinced ourselves that we should be able to negotiate our salary entirely from memory while our nervous system is in crisis mode, which is setting ourselves up for failure.

The stomach-drop sensation that some of us experience is connected to the vagus nerve, which runs from the brain through the chest and abdomen and is heavily involved in the stress response. When the vagus nerve activates in response to perceived threat, it can cause that falling-elevator feeling in our stomach, along with nausea in some cases. This is pure physiology, not psychological weakness, and it's one of the more unpleasant aspects of negotiation anxiety because it's hard to think clearly when we feel like we might throw up. The sensation usually peaks in the first few minutes of a stressful conversation and then subsides somewhat as the body adjusts, which means if we can get through the initial moments without bolting, it often becomes more manageable even though it doesn't disappear completely.

Breathing changes during stress are another visible marker that can create self-consciousness. Our breathing gets faster and shallower as part of the fight-or-flight response, which makes sense if we need to run but doesn't help when we need to speak clearly and think strategically. Shallow breathing also tends to increase anxiety rather than decrease it because it signals to our body that we're still in danger, creating another reinforcing loop. The intervention here is deliberately slowing our breathing before and during the conversation, which sounds like generic mindfulness advice but actually has a measurable physiological effect on vagal tone and stress hormone levels. Taking three slow breaths before responding to an offer or before starting a raise conversation does genuinely help, not by eliminating anxiety but by preventing it from escalating into full panic.

Some people experience a kind of tunnel vision or auditory narrowing during high-stress moments where they can see and hear the person in front of them but peripheral information drops away and the world feels narrower than usual. This is the stress response directing our attention to the immediate perceived threat and filtering out everything else, which again makes sense for physical danger but is counterproductive in negotiation where we need to be tracking multiple pieces of information and thinking through implications. When this happens during a salary conversation, we might miss cues about flexibility in the other person's position or fail to notice opportunities to negotiate components other than base salary because our attention has narrowed too much to process anything beyond the immediate exchange.

Recognizing this narrowing when it happens is difficult because by definition we're not aware of what we're not processing, but we can prepare for it by having notes that explicitly list other compensation components to discuss if salary is constrained. When our attention narrows, we can look at the list and force ourselves to consider options that wouldn't naturally occur to us in that mental state. This is another form of externalizing cognitive load from our stressed brain to systems and documents that don't stop working under pressure.

The crying response is probably the most feared physical manifestation of negotiation stress, especially for women who already worry about being stereotyped as too emotional in professional settings. Crying during negotiation isn't common but it's not rare either, and it happens for the same reason as all the other physical symptoms: the stress response has triggered emotional reactivity that bypasses our conscious control. Some people cry when they're frustrated, some when they're angry, some when they feel cornered or misunderstood, and the specific trigger doesn't really matter because the underlying mechanism is the same loss of emotional regulation under stress.

If crying happens during a negotiation, the worst thing we can do is apologize profusely and shut down the conversation, which is what most of us instinctively want to do because we're embarrassed. The better response is brief acknowledgment without dwelling on it, something like "I get emotional in high-stakes conversations, I'm fine, let's keep going," and then continuing with the substance of what we were saying. This is extraordinarily hard to execute when we're already upset and now also embarrassed about being upset, but it's effective because it refuses to let the crying become the focus and instead treats it as a minor side effect that doesn't change the validity of what we're requesting. Most people who witness someone crying during a professional conversation are themselves uncomfortable and looking for cues about how to respond, and if we signal that we're moving forward, they'll usually follow that lead rather than making a bigger deal of it.

The range of physical responses people experience during negotiation stress is wide enough that almost everyone has something that makes them self-conscious or worried about being perceived as weak or incompetent. Some people sweat visibly. Some people's hands shake when holding papers. Some people develop a stress headache that makes it hard to concentrate. Some people feel dizzy or lightheaded. Some people get an urgent need to use the bathroom. All of these are normal stress responses, and none of them mean we shouldn't negotiate, they just mean we need to work with our particular physiology rather than pretending we can simply override it through determination.

Planning for our specific physical responses makes them less derailing when they show up. If we know our hands shake, we don't hold papers during the conversation, we keep them on the table or in our lap where the shaking is less visible. If we know we get stress headaches, we take ibuprofen beforehand rather than trying to push through the pain. If we know we need to use the bathroom when nervous, we go right before the conversation starts even if we don't feel an urgent need yet. These are tiny adjustments but they remove one source of distraction from a situation that's already demanding all our focus.

The fundamental point that needs to keep coming back is that none of these physical responses are character flaws or signs that we're not cut out for negotiation. They're evolutionary adaptations that kept our ancestors alive in environments where social rejection actually was life-threatening. Our bodies are doing exactly what they're designed to do when faced with perceived social danger, and the fact that salary negotiation in 2024 isn't actually dangerous doesn't change the ancient wiring that produces the response. We're not trying to become people who don't have stress responses. We're trying to negotiate successfully despite having them, and that's achievable through preparation and structure and accepting our physiology as something to work with rather than something to be ashamed of.

# The Truth behind Numbers

When we're staring at a job offer for $68,000 and trying to decide whether to negotiate for $73,000, what we see is a difference of $5,000, which feels meaningful but not exactly life-changing. We're not thinking about decades or compound returns or how this number becomes the anchor for every future conversation about our compensation. We're thinking about whether $5,000 is worth the discomfort of asking, and when framed that way, the answer often lands on "probably not," which is how most of us end up leaving massive amounts of money on the table without ever quite realizing what we did.

The actual calculation looks nothing like the mental math we do in the moment. That $5,000 difference at age 25 doesn't stay $5,000. Assuming standard annual raises of 3%, which is roughly average across industries, the person who started at $73,000 is making $76,190 after year two while the person who started at $68,000 is making $71,080. The gap has grown from $5,000 to $5,110 just from raises, and this gap continues expanding every year because each raise is a percentage of the base, not a flat amount. After five years, the gap is $6,630 annually. After ten years, it's $8,612 annually. After twenty years, it's $11,185 annually. After thirty years, it's $14,530 annually.

Adding up just the salary differences over 30 years, without considering investment returns or retirement contributions or bonuses, the person who negotiated their first offer makes $289,163 more than the person who didn't. That's the floor of what we lose by not having one fifteen-minute conversation at age 25, and it's already enough to pay off most mortgages or fund a child's entire college education or retire three years earlier, but it's not even close to the actual long-term cost because most of us don't just collect salary and spend it all, at least some of it gets invested in retirement accounts where compound returns do their work.

If we take that same scenario and assume the person who negotiated puts the extra $5,000 into a retirement account in year one, plus the additional difference each subsequent year, and assume a 7% annual return which is conservative for long-term stock market performance, the account balance at age 65 ends up at $634,418. The person who didn't negotiate and therefore didn't have that extra money to invest ends up with $634,418 less in retirement savings, which is the difference between retiring comfortably at 65 and working until 70, or the difference between retiring at all and working indefinitely because the math doesn't close otherwise.

This is the number nobody shows us when we're sitting with that job offer trying to decide whether to negotiate. We see $68,000 versus $73,000 and we think we're choosing between two salary numbers, when what we're actually choosing is whether to have $634,418 more in retirement or not. The cognitive distance between these two framings is so extreme that they barely feel like the same decision, and because we can't see the compound effects in the moment, we optimize for immediate comfort rather than long-term financial security.

The pattern repeats at every job change and every raise negotiation throughout a career, which is how the numbers get even more severe than the single scenario suggests. Most people change jobs seven to ten times over their working life, and each time they accept an offer without negotiating, they're not just losing the difference for that year, they're resetting the baseline lower than it should be for every subsequent conversation. A person who consistently negotiates every offer and every raise ends up on a completely different trajectory than someone who accepts first offers and waits for employers to proactively increase their pay, which employers rarely do beyond cost-of-living adjustments.

Women who negotiate consistently throughout their careers earn between $1,000,000 and $1,500,000 more over a lifetime than women who don't, according to multiple longitudinal studies tracking MBA graduates and professional workers across decades. This isn't from landing one massive salary or getting lucky with a big promotion. This is pure accumulation from negotiating starting salaries, negotiating raises, negotiating offers when changing jobs, and treating compensation as something that requires active management rather than something that happens to us based on employer generosity. The women who end up $1,000,000 ahead aren't necessarily more talented or harder working than the women who don't negotiate. They're just having conversations the others are avoiding, and those conversations stack over time in ways that become impossible to catch up with later.

The gender pay gap statistics make more sense when we understand compounding. Women earn roughly 84 cents for every dollar men earn when we look at median wages across all workers, and this gap has barely moved in the past fifteen years despite enormous amounts of attention and corporate diversity initiatives. Part of this comes from occupational segregation and part comes from women taking time out of the workforce for caregiving, but a meaningful chunk comes from negotiation patterns that start small and compound over decades. Women MBA graduates earn 88% of what male graduates earn in their first job out of school, which is already a gap but not a catastrophic one, and then ten years later they're earning 63% of what men earn, which is the gap widening through accumulated smaller decisions rather than one dramatic moment of discrimination.

Each of those smaller decisions looks defensible in isolation. Taking a slightly lower offer to avoid conflict seems reasonable when it's only $4,000 less. Not pushing for a raise this year because we got one last year seems prudent. Accepting the "this is really our best offer" statement without exploring other compensation options seems realistic. But these decisions don't exist in isolation, they build on each other and create a salary history that follows us everywhere, and by year ten we're looking at a gap that feels impossible to close through normal raise cycles because we'd need sustained 15-20% annual increases just to catch up to where we should have been.

The compounding works in reverse too, which is why one successful negotiation early in a career has disproportionate impact compared to negotiating later. A 25-year-old who negotiates a $5,000 increase builds wealth on that base for 40 years. A 45-year-old who negotiates the same $5,000 increase only builds on it for 20 years. The raw dollar difference is identical but the compound effect is roughly half, which means the cost of not negotiating early is something we can never fully recover from later. We can still catch up somewhat through aggressive job changes and strategic moves, but we'll always be behind where we would have been if we'd negotiated from the beginning.

Most of us don't think about raises as compounding events, we think about them as annual bumps that either happen or don't based on performance. The typical raise cycle works like this: once a year, usually around annual review time, our manager submits a salary increase recommendation to HR, HR either approves it or adjusts it based on budget constraints, and we get a letter saying our salary is increasing by 3% or maybe 5% if we had a particularly good year. This process is presented as if it's merit-based and tied to our performance, and sometimes it genuinely is, but more often it's constrained by whatever percentage increase HR has allocated to each department, and those percentages rarely account for market rate changes or individual negotiation history.

What this means practically is that if we started $7,000 below where we should have been, and we get consistent 3% raises every year, we never catch up to the trajectory we should have been on. After ten years of 3% raises starting from $68,000, we're at $88,403. After ten years of 3% raises starting from $73,000, we're at $94,890. The gap has actually grown from $5,000 to $6,487 just through standard raise mechanics, and this gap continues expanding forever unless something breaks the pattern. The way to break the pattern is either to negotiate a larger-than-normal raise, which requires making a case for why we deserve to jump ahead of the standard percentage, or to change jobs and negotiate the new offer aggressively, which resets the baseline but also requires the same negotiation skills we're trying to avoid.

Bonuses compound similarly when they're calculated as a percentage of base salary. A 10% bonus on $68,000 is $6,800, while a 10% bonus on $73,000 is $7,300. That's $500 less per year in bonus money alone, which over thirty years at the same 7% investment return becomes roughly $47,250 less in retirement savings. Stock options, when they're part of compensation packages, often scale with salary level too, which means a lower base salary results in fewer options or lower-value grants. 401k matches are almost always a percentage of contribution, and contributions are capped as a percentage of salary, so a lower salary means less match money even if we're contributing the same percentage of our income. Every component of compensation that ties to base salary magnifies the initial negotiation gap.

The invisibility of these effects is part of why we keep making the same mistake. We accept an offer, we get our paychecks, we see money showing up in our account, and nothing feels wrong because we're not comparing ourselves to what we could have had, we're comparing ourselves to what we had before. The counterfactual earnings don't show up anywhere on our pay stub or bank statement. We never see the line item that says "amount you would have made if you'd negotiated" because that number doesn't exist in any system we interact with. The only way to know we left money on the table is to do the math ourselves, and most of us never do that calculation because it's depressing to realize how much we lost.

Some of us avoid this calculation on purpose because knowing the number would feel worse than not knowing. There's a certain protection in vagueness, where we can tell ourselves it probably wasn't that much and we made the choice we needed to make given our circumstances and discomfort level, without confronting the actual six-figure consequences of letting anxiety drive our decisions. This is understandable as a coping mechanism but it doesn't change the underlying reality, which is that the money we didn't negotiate for is still gone, whether we calculate it precisely or not.

The retirement gap deserves particular attention because it's where the compound effects become most severe and most concrete. A person who consistently earns 10% less than they should throughout their career, which is roughly what happens when we never negotiate, doesn't just retire with 10% less savings. They retire with 40-50% less savings because those earnings would have been invested for decades and grown through compound returns. The difference between a comfortable retirement and a precarious one often comes down to whether someone negotiated their salary consistently throughout their twenties and thirties, which is exactly when most of us were least equipped to do it because we were still learning how work and money and professional relationships function.

Social Security benefits in the United States are calculated based on lifetime earnings, specifically the highest 35 years of indexed earnings. Lower salary throughout our career means lower Social Security benefits in retirement, which is another compounding effect that doesn't show up in any immediate calculation but meaningfully affects our financial security for the last 20-30 years of our life. A 10% lower lifetime earnings average could mean $200-300 less per month in Social Security benefits, which sounds small until we multiply it by 25 years of retirement and realize it's $60,000-90,000 in lost benefits.

The math here isn't presented as motivation or as a way to make us feel bad about past decisions we can't change. It's presented as information we need to make clear decisions going forward. Knowing that one negotiation compounds to $634,000 over a career doesn't mean we're bad with money if we didn't negotiate in the past. It means the next time we're looking at an offer and trying to decide whether fifteen minutes of discomfort is worth it, we have actual numbers to weigh against the anxiety, and those numbers are significant enough that they might shift the calculation from "not worth it" to "worth it even though it's terrible."

The financial stakes are real and large and measurable, and pretending they're not doesn't make them go away, it just means we're making decisions without full information about what those decisions cost us.

The lifecycle of salary decisions matters more than any single number because each decision sets the baseline for the next one. When we accept our first job offer at $68,000 instead of negotiating to $73,000, we're not just taking $5,000 less that year. We're establishing $68,000 as our salary history, which becomes the anchor point for our next job search or internal raise request. Most companies, when making offers or considering raises, look at what we're currently making or most recently made and use that as the starting point for their calculations. Some add a percentage on top, some add a flat amount, but almost all of them treat our previous salary as relevant information about what we should be paid next.

This anchoring effect means that accepting a low offer early in our career creates drag on our earning potential for years or even decades afterward. When we're 27 and looking for our second job, potential employers ask what we're currently making. If we say $68,000, they might offer $76,000, thinking they're giving us a solid 12% increase. If we'd started at $73,000, that same percentage increase logic would put us at $81,760. The gap has widened from $5,000 to $5,760 just from normal job-hopping progression, and this pattern continues through every subsequent move. By the time we're 35 and on our fourth or fifth job, we're looking at offers that are $15,000 to $20,000 lower than they would have been if we'd negotiated that first position.

Some states and cities have banned the practice of asking about salary history specifically to break this cycle, recognizing that it perpetuates pay gaps and punishes people who accepted low initial offers. California, Colorado, Connecticut, Delaware, Hawaii, Illinois, Maine, Maryland, Massachusetts, Oregon, Vermont, and Washington have various forms of salary history bans as of 2024, along with cities like New York City, Philadelphia, and Pittsburgh. In these locations, employers can't ask what we made before and can't use that information even if they somehow obtain it. This is helpful for people starting their careers in those places or moving there from elsewhere, but it doesn't eliminate the problem entirely because we still carry our own internal anchor about what we're worth based on what we've been paid, and that affects how we negotiate even when employers can't explicitly ask.

The psychology of anchoring works on us even when we know it's happening, which is one of the more frustrating aspects of how human decision-making operates. Research on anchoring effects shows that even completely arbitrary numbers influence subsequent judgments. In one famous study, people were asked whether Gandhi died before or after age 114, then asked to estimate his actual age at death. People given the 114 anchor estimated significantly higher ages than people given a lower anchor, even though everyone knew 114 was absurd. Our own salary history operates as a much more powerful anchor than random numbers because it feels like meaningful information about our market value, even when we know logically that our previous employer might have underpaid us or that we accepted less than we should have.

Breaking free from this anchor requires deliberate effort to research current market rates and base our negotiations on that external data rather than on our personal history. This is psychologically difficult because it means asking for amounts that might be 20% or 30% higher than what we're currently making, which feels aggressive or unrealistic even when it's exactly what the market pays for our skills and experience. The discomfort of asking for a large percentage increase often causes us to moderate our request down to something that feels more reasonable relative to our current salary, which is the anchor pulling us back down even though we're consciously trying to ignore it.

Job changes are the primary opportunities most of us have to reset our salary trajectory because internal raises rarely exceed 5-10% even for strong performers, while job changes can yield 15-30% increases if negotiated properly. This is why career advice often emphasizes job hopping every two to four years in early career stages, not because loyalty is bad but because the financial math strongly favors strategic movement. Someone who stays at one company for eight years and gets 3% annual raises ends up roughly 26% higher than their starting salary. Someone who changes jobs twice in that same eight years and negotiates 20% increases each time ends up 44% higher than their starting salary, nearly double the gain for the same time period.

The compound effects of job change increases are dramatic enough that they overcome almost any argument about the value of staying put for stability or advancement opportunities. Even if we love our current job and feel loyalty to our team, the financial cost of staying is high enough that it needs to be a conscious choice made with full awareness of what we're giving up rather than a passive decision driven by inertia or discomfort with job searching. This isn't an argument that everyone should constantly job hop, it's an observation that the pay structures of most organizations punish loyalty and reward movement, which means staying needs to be actively worth it in non-financial ways.

Some companies have recognized this pattern and implemented policies to match external offers when valued employees announce they're leaving, but this creates its own dysfunctional dynamic where we effectively have to threaten to quit in order to get paid fairly. Playing this game is risky because sometimes the company will call the bluff and let us go, leaving us with no current job and a potentially awkward situation if the external offer wasn't as firm as we thought it was. The healthier pattern is treating job changes as strategic opportunities to reset our compensation baseline rather than as hostage negotiation where we leverage outside offers to extract fair pay from current employers.

The retirement savings gap that results from salary gaps is where the long-term cost becomes most concrete and most severe. Most retirement savings in the United States happens through employer-sponsored 401k plans, and the maximum we can contribute in 2024 is $23,000 per year for people under 50. That's an absolute cap regardless of salary, which sounds like it would make salary differences irrelevant for retirement savings, but it doesn't work that way in practice because most people don't contribute the maximum and because employer matches are calculated as a percentage of salary.

A typical employer 401k match is 50% of employee contributions up to 6% of salary. For someone making $68,000 and contributing 6%, that's $4,080 in employee contribution and $2,040 in employer match, for a total of $6,120 going into retirement accounts annually. For someone making $73,000 at the same contribution rate, that's $4,380 in employee contribution and $2,190 in employer match, for a total of $6,570 annually. The difference is $450 per year in retirement contributions, which over 30 years at 7% annual returns becomes approximately $42,600. That's just from the employer match differential, not accounting for the fact that the person earning more also has more disposable income to potentially save beyond the match percentage.

Many people don't contribute enough to get the full employer match because the paycheck reduction feels too tight relative to their immediate expenses, which means the lower our salary, the less likely we are to maximize even the free money that employers are offering. Someone making $68,000 might contribute 3% because 6% feels like too much to give up from their monthly budget, which means they're leaving employer match money on the table. Someone making $73,000 has more room in their budget and might contribute the full 6%, capturing the entire match. This creates a double penalty where lower salary results in both smaller total contributions and missed employer matching funds.

The catch-up contributions allowed for people over 50, currently an additional $7,500 per year, were designed to help people who under-saved earlier in their careers make up some ground, but they can't fully compensate for decades of lower savings rates. Someone who was $10,000 behind in salary from age 25 to 50 and therefore saved less throughout that period would need to contribute substantially more from 50 to 65 to catch up, but their salary in those later years is also probably still lower than it would have been if they'd negotiated early, which means they still have less income available for increased contributions. The compounding disadvantage is very hard to overcome once it's been building for multiple decades.

Social Security benefits add another layer to the retirement income gap because they're calculated based on lifetime earnings. The Social Security Administration averages our highest 35 years of indexed earnings and uses that average to determine our benefit amount. Someone who earned less throughout their career because they didn't negotiate receives lower Social Security benefits in retirement, and unlike savings accounts where we can potentially catch up through aggressive saving later, Social Security benefits are purely a function of what we earned when we were working. There's no way to retroactively increase them by saving more after retirement.

The benefit reduction from consistently lower earnings is not trivial. Social Security benefits max out at around $3,800 per month in 2024 for someone who consistently earned at or above the Social Security wage base throughout their career. Someone who earned 10% less throughout their career receives roughly 10% less in benefits, which is $380 per month or $4,560 per year. Over a 25-year retirement, that's $114,000 in reduced benefits that we can't make up through personal savings because Social Security is a separate system with its own rules. This reduction happens regardless of how much we have in personal retirement accounts, which means even if we somehow managed to save aggressively enough to overcome the salary differential, we're still receiving less from Social Security forever.

Healthcare costs in retirement interact with this gap in ways that compound the disadvantage. Medicare has premiums and copays and doesn't cover everything, which means retirees need supplemental insurance and out-of-pocket funds for medical expenses. Someone with lower lifetime earnings has both lower Social Security income and lower retirement savings to cover these costs, while their healthcare needs are likely similar to or higher than someone who earned more, since health problems don't correlate neatly with income. The result is that financial stress in retirement is significantly higher for people who consistently accepted lower compensation throughout their working years, not by a small margin but by enough to affect their quality of life and their options for care.

The numbers we've been walking through assume relatively conservative investment returns of 7% annually, which is below the long-term stock market average of around 10% but above what we'd get from safer investments like bonds. If we assume higher returns, the compound effects are even more dramatic. At 10% returns, that $5,000 salary difference compounded over 30 years becomes roughly $987,000 instead of $634,000. At 5% returns, it's still $398,000. The exact number varies with market conditions and investment choices, but the principle holds across reasonable assumptions: small salary differences early in our career compound into massive wealth differences later.

These calculations also assume we invest the additional income rather than spending it, which is obviously not automatic. The person who negotiates for $73,000 instead of $68,000 doesn't magically have $634,000 more in retirement if they spend the extra $5,000 every year on a nicer apartment or more expensive car. The compound effect only works if the money actually gets invested and stays invested rather than being consumed immediately. This is why having a plan for what we'll do with negotiated increases matters almost as much as getting the increases in the first place, but that's a separate conversation about financial discipline rather than about negotiation itself.

What we can say with confidence is that negotiation creates the option to build wealth through compound returns, while not negotiating eliminates that option by reducing the resources we have available to invest. Someone making $68,000 might be able to save $5,000 per year after expenses. Someone making $73,000 might be able to save $10,000 per year because they've covered their baseline expenses and now the marginal dollars are purely discretionary. The difference in savings rate is often higher than the difference in salary, which means small salary increases can enable disproportionately large increases in wealth accumulation.

# What We Were Taught About Money and Asking

Most of us absorbed messages about money and asking for things before we had language to question whether those messages were accurate or helpful, which means they operate as background assumptions rather than conscious beliefs we can examine and potentially discard. The specific messages vary by family and culture and class background, but they cluster around similar themes: talking about money is impolite, asking for more makes us look greedy, people who focus on compensation care about the wrong things, and we should be grateful for what we're offered rather than pushing for more. These ideas get reinforced through years of small interactions and observations until they feel like facts about how the world works rather than opinions some adults had about appropriate behavior, and then we carry them into salary negotiations where they sabotage us in ways we don't fully recognize at the time.

The "money talk is vulgar" message shows up across different economic backgrounds, though the reasoning shifts. In families with money, discussing specific amounts was often treated as crass or showing off, something people with breeding didn't do because it reduced relationships to transactions. In families without money, discussing amounts was painful because it highlighted scarcity and limitation, which meant the polite thing was to avoid the topic entirely rather than making everyone uncomfortable by naming what wasn't there. Both versions taught us that talking explicitly about compensation is somehow inappropriate or aggressive, which makes salary negotiation feel like we're violating a social norm rather than engaging in standard business practice.

When we were children asking parents for things, the dynamic was fundamentally about power imbalance, and that dynamic gets reactivated when we're sitting across from a hiring manager even though the situations aren't actually comparable. Asking our parents for a toy or permission to do something meant putting ourselves in a vulnerable position where they had complete authority to say yes or no, and when they said no it often came with judgment about whether we should have asked in the first place, whether we were being spoiled or ungrateful, whether we understood how hard they worked to provide what we already had. Those memories encode as "asking for things risks rejection plus moral judgment about our character," which is approximately the worst possible frame for salary negotiation because it makes the conversation about our worth as a person rather than about market rates and value exchange.

The difference that should be obvious but often isn't: parents deciding whether to buy us something was actually about their resources and priorities and values, while employers deciding whether to pay us more is supposed to be about market rates and budget and what we bring to the role. These are completely different calculations, but if we're operating from childhood patterns, we experience the hiring manager's evaluation as equivalent to a parent deciding whether we deserve what we're asking for, and that framing makes it nearly impossible to negotiate with any kind of clarity or confidence.

Women get an additional layer of messaging around accommodation and not making waves that compounds the general money discomfort. Girls are socialized from very early to be aware of other people's comfort and to prioritize harmony over their own needs, which gets reinforced through thousands of small interactions where being assertive gets coded as bossy or difficult while the same behavior in boys gets coded as leadership potential. This isn't a conspiracy or anyone's deliberate plan, it's just how gendered socialization works through accumulated micro-messages that add up to very clear instructions about what kind of behavior is acceptable and what kind will result in social penalties. By the time we're adults in the workplace, we've had twenty-plus years of feedback that being accommodating and easy to work with is how we maintain relationships and that pushing for what we want risks being seen as unlikable, and unlikability for women has career costs that it doesn't have for men.

The research on this is uncomfortably clear. When women negotiate in ways that men negotiate with no penalty, women face backlash that shows up as being rated less hirable, less likable, less desirable as colleagues, and less likely to be chosen for collaborative projects. This isn't perception bias on our part or oversensitivity to feedback, this is measurable difference in how identical behavior gets evaluated based on gender. Men who advocate for higher salary are seen as appropriately assertive and confident. Women who advocate for the same salary are seen as demanding and not team players. The stereotype that women are bad at negotiation or don't negotiate enough has been proven wrong by recent studies showing women now negotiate at higher rates than men, 54% versus 44% in MBA graduate populations, but women still earn less because when we negotiate we get told no more often.

This creates an impossible situation where the standard advice to negotiate doesn't account for the fact that following that advice has different costs depending on who's doing it. A woman who negotiates might get a better salary in the immediate term but also might get marked as difficult in ways that affect her trajectory over the next several years. A woman who doesn't negotiate avoids the immediate social penalty but falls behind financially in ways that compound over time. There's no clean answer here because the problem isn't individual behavior, it's systemic bias in how behavior gets interpreted, but most career advice is written as if the playing field is level and we just need to learn the right techniques.

Class background affects negotiation comfort in ways that rarely get discussed in career literature, probably because most career advice is written by and for people who had some economic security growing up. People who grew up without money or with precarious financial situations often have much higher anxiety about losing opportunities than people who grew up with safety nets. If we're the first in our family to have a professional job, or if we remember what it felt like when there wasn't enough money for basic needs, the risk of an offer being rescinded because we negotiated feels genuinely dangerous in ways that are hard to explain to someone who's never experienced that kind of financial precarity. The advice to "know your worth" and "don't settle" assumes we have the luxury of walking away from opportunities that aren't perfect, but for many of us, walking away isn't a real option when we have student loans and family members who depend on us and no backup plan if this job disappears.

Impostor syndrome layers on top of all of this and makes negotiation feel like exposing ourselves as frauds. If we already suspect we don't fully deserve to be in the room or that we somehow got the opportunity through luck rather than merit, asking for more money feels like inviting closer scrutiny that will reveal we're not actually qualified for what we're being offered in the first place. The logic becomes circular: if I were really worth more money they would have offered it, the fact that they didn't offer it means I'm probably already at the high end of what I'm worth, if I ask for more I'm claiming value I don't actually have, and they'll realize they made a mistake in offering me anything at all. This thought pattern is completely disconnected from how hiring and compensation actually work, but impostor syndrome doesn't care about reality, it cares about protecting us from potential exposure by keeping us small and quiet and grateful.

The combination of these messages creates a situation where negotiation feels morally wrong rather than just uncomfortable. We're not thinking "this is an unpleasant but normal business conversation," we're thinking "I'm being greedy, I'm making this person uncomfortable, I'm violating social norms about politeness, I'm risking everything by not being sufficiently grateful for what's being offered, and I probably don't even deserve what I'm asking for anyway." With that much internal resistance operating underneath the surface conversation, it's almost impressive that anyone manages to negotiate at all.

What makes this particularly difficult to untangle is that some of these patterns served us well in childhood even though they harm us now. Being attuned to adult moods and adjusting our behavior to maintain harmony kept many of us safe in households where conflict was dangerous or where parental approval was conditional. Learning to not ask for things we wouldn't get anyway saved us from repeated rejection and helped us manage disappointment. Accepting what was offered without pushing for more made us easier to deal with and might have protected us from being seen as demanding or difficult. These were reasonable adaptations to the environments we were in, and the fact that they're now costing us money doesn't mean we were wrong to develop them.

The work isn't to judge ourselves for having these patterns but to recognize them clearly enough that we can make conscious decisions about when to follow them and when to override them. In our personal relationships, maybe being accommodating and avoiding conflict still serves us well. In salary negotiations, those same instincts leave hundreds of thousands of dollars on the table, which means we need different operating instructions for this specific context even if we keep the old patterns everywhere else.

Some of us grew up with parents who modeled negotiation as a normal part of life, who negotiated car prices and medical bills and salaries and taught us through observation that asking for better terms is standard practice rather than something to be ashamed of. Those of us who had that modeling have an enormous advantage because we're not fighting against years of messaging that negotiation is inappropriate. We saw it work, we saw it didn't destroy relationships, we saw that most of the time people expect it and aren't offended by it. Those of us who didn't get that modeling have to build the permission from scratch, which is harder but not impossible.

The specific childhood memories that get triggered in negotiations are often surprisingly mundane but viscerally uncomfortable. Asking dad for money for a school trip and seeing him get angry about having to provide one more thing. Asking mom if we could get something at the store and hearing that long sigh that meant we were being too much. Asking for something and being told "we can't afford it" in a tone that also communicated "and it's stressful that you don't understand that." These weren't necessarily bad parents or traumatic events, they were just normal family dynamics around limited resources, but they taught us that asking puts strain on relationships and that the considerate thing is to not ask unless absolutely necessary.

Salary negotiation isn't absolutely necessary in the same way childhood needs were, which means our childhood programming tells us it's optional and we should skip it to avoid putting strain on the relationship before it's even started. The problem with this logic is that employer-employee relationships aren't parent-child relationships, employers actually expect negotiation and budget for it, and not negotiating signals either that we don't know what we're worth or that we're not serious about the role. The strain we're trying to avoid by not negotiating isn't actually a risk in professional contexts the way it was in childhood contexts, but our nervous system doesn't distinguish between the two because the emotional flavor is similar enough to trigger the old patterns.

Breaking these patterns doesn't require therapy or deep psychological work, though those things might help in broader ways. What it requires is naming them explicitly so we can see them as learned behavior rather than objective truth, and then building new scripts that override the old programming in this specific context. We don't need to become people who are comfortable asking for things in all situations. We need to be able to execute one type of business conversation even though everything in our background is telling us not to, and that's achievable with enough preparation and structure even if it never stops feeling uncomfortable at a gut level.

The messages we absorbed about money and asking don't disappear just because we understand where they came from or recognize they're not serving us anymore. They show up in the moment as physical resistance and emotional discomfort and voices in our head saying we're being inappropriate or greedy or too much. Knowing the messages are there doesn't neutralize them, but it does give us room to act despite them instead of treating them as accurate information about whether we should negotiate.

The specific ways these messages manifest during actual negotiations are predictable enough that we can prepare for them rather than being ambushed. When we're about to ask for more money, a voice will likely tell us we're being greedy, and we can recognize that as childhood programming about gratitude rather than accurate assessment of our request. When we feel guilty about negotiating, we can identify that as the people-pleasing instinct that was useful in childhood but costs us money now. When we worry that the hiring manager will think less of us for asking, we can separate that from the reality that professional negotiation is expected and normal.

The work of separating these internalized messages from current reality is ongoing rather than something we do once and then it's solved. Each new negotiation will trigger the same old patterns because they're deeply embedded in how we process social interactions involving money and power. The difference is that over time we get better at recognizing the patterns quickly and moving forward despite them rather than being completely controlled by them. The discomfort doesn't diminish much, but our ability to act despite discomfort improves with practice.

Different cultural backgrounds add specific overlays to the general money discomfort that most of us carry. In some Asian cultures, modesty and indirectness around self-promotion are valued highly, which makes the American style of salary negotiation feel particularly jarring and inappropriate. In some Latin American cultures, strong emphasis on relationship harmony and respect for authority makes pushing back on an employer's offer feel disrespectful. In many European cultures, salary is considered private to the point where discussing it even with colleagues is taboo, which makes researching market rates harder and makes negotiation feel like we're being too American in our approach.

These cultural messages aren't wrong in their original context, but they create friction when we're operating in professional environments that expect negotiation regardless of our cultural background. Someone who grew up in a culture where questioning authority is considered rude doesn't suddenly develop comfort with challenging an offer just because they're now working at an American company. The tension between our cultural training and the expectations of the workplace we're in creates an additional layer of stress beyond what people whose cultural background aligns with dominant American business norms experience.

First-generation professionals, meaning people who are the first in their family to have white-collar careers, face particular difficulties with negotiation because we often lack models for how these conversations work and what's considered normal versus inappropriate. Our parents might have worked hourly jobs where negotiation wasn't an option or small business environments where everything was informal and relationship-based rather than structured around market rates and formal offers. We don't have memories of watching a parent negotiate a salary increase or hearing dinner table conversations about whether a job offer was competitive. We're figuring out the norms from scratch, which makes every decision feel high-stakes because we're not sure if what we're doing is standard practice or a serious violation of unspoken rules.

The pressure to not mess up opportunities is intense for first-generation professionals because we're often supporting family members financially or emotionally and because the job represents not just our own economic security but proof that the family's sacrifices and investments in our education paid off. Risking an offer by negotiating feels irresponsible when so much is riding on our success, which means we're much more likely to accept whatever's offered rather than push for more. This is rational risk management given our circumstances, but it also means we end up on lower salary trajectories than peers who have more family wealth and support to fall back on if something goes wrong.

The immigrant experience adds another dimension where negotiation might feel like drawing negative attention to ourselves at a time when staying under the radar feels safer. For people on work visas, job loss means having to leave the country, which makes any negotiation that could theoretically jeopardize the offer feel genuinely dangerous in ways that citizens don't experience. Even for people who are legally secure in their status, having grown up navigating systems that weren't built for us often creates habits around not making waves and not asking for things that might mark us as difficult. These habits served a protective function but cost us money in contexts where assertiveness is expected and rewarded.

Gender socialization around money and work is specific enough that it deserves separate examination beyond the general negotiation backlash we discussed earlier. Girls are often raised with messaging that their future financial security will come through partnership rather than their own earning power, which means investing heavily in salary negotiation feels less urgent than it actually is. This messaging has shifted dramatically in recent decades, but it's still present in subtle ways, particularly in families where mothers weren't primary earners or where traditional gender roles were strongly modeled. The implicit assumption that our income is supplementary rather than essential makes negotiation feel optional when it's actually critical to our long-term independence and security.

Women are also socialized to consider how our career choices affect our future ability to have children and manage household responsibilities, which introduces calculations that men rarely have to think about in the same way. When we're evaluating a job offer, we're not just thinking about salary and growth potential, we're thinking about flexibility for future parenting, whether the company culture supports working mothers, how much travel is required, whether the hours would be compatible with childcare arrangements. These are legitimate considerations, but they sometimes result in accepting lower compensation in exchange for perceived flexibility, and that trade-off compounds over time in ways that significantly affect lifetime earnings.

The mommy track phenomenon, where women with children or who are perceived as likely to have children get sidelined from advancement opportunities, interacts with negotiation in ways that create additional barriers. Women who negotiate aggressively early in their careers sometimes find themselves penalized later when they have children because the assertiveness that was already viewed somewhat negatively becomes even more problematic once they're mothers. The stereotype of the demanding mother who won't be fully committed to work creates pressure to be extra accommodating and grateful rather than continuing to negotiate for fair compensation and advancement.

Male socialization around money and work creates its own problems that manifest differently. Men who are raised with expectations that they'll be primary earners carry enormous pressure to achieve financially, which can make negotiation feel mandatory rather than optional but also creates intense anxiety about job loss or failure to meet income expectations. Men who experience this pressure sometimes overcompensate by becoming overly aggressive in negotiations or by taking jobs primarily based on salary without considering other factors that affect quality of life and long-term career sustainability.

Men who are naturally conflict-averse or introverted face a particular kind of shame around negotiation difficulty because it conflicts with masculine expectations about assertiveness and competitiveness. The messaging is that real men don't struggle with these conversations, they confidently demand what they're worth and walk away if they don't get it. Men who find negotiation terrifying often hide that terror more carefully than women do because admitting it feels like admitting inadequacy as men, which creates isolation and prevents them from seeking help or acknowledging that they need different strategies than what standard advice assumes.

The relationship between money and self-worth that many of us develop in childhood, regardless of gender, becomes problematic when we're negotiating compensation because we conflate what we're paid with what we're worth as people. This is a category error that's easy to identify intellectually but very hard to shake emotionally. When a hiring manager offers us $68,000 and we were hoping for $75,000, our emotional brain processes this as "they think I'm worth $68,000" which then becomes "I'm only worth $68,000" which then makes asking for more feel like lying about our value. The fact that salary is actually about market rates and budget allocations and negotiation norms rather than a precise measure of our human worth doesn't change how it feels when we're in the conversation.

Breaking the connection between salary and self-worth requires actively reminding ourselves that these are separate categories. We are worth infinite value as humans. Our labor is worth whatever the market pays for our particular skills and experience in our particular location at this particular time. These are not the same thing, but they feel like the same thing when we're sitting across from someone who's putting a specific dollar amount on hiring us. The practice of separating the two happens through internal dialogue that we have to initiate deliberately rather than waiting for it to feel natural, saying to ourselves "this number is about market rates not about me as a person" repeatedly until it starts to create some emotional distance from the equation.

Some of us had parents who were overly focused on money as a measure of success, which created its own distortions where we learned that our value to them was partly determined by our earning potential. This might show up as pressure to choose high-paying careers regardless of our interests, or as parents bragging about our salaries to relatives, or as implicit competition with siblings around who's earning more. When we've been raised to equate income with parental approval and family status, negotiation becomes even more fraught because it's not just about our financial security, it's about proving we're successful enough to be valued by our family.

The opposite pattern, where parents dismissed money as unimportant or vulgar and emphasized that good people don't care about material things, creates different problems. We might have internalized that caring about our salary means we're shallow or materialistic, which makes negotiation feel like we're betraying our values. This is particularly common among people raised in religious or artistic or academic families where money was treated as necessary but somewhat distasteful, something to be managed minimally rather than pursued or discussed openly. Asking for more money then feels like admitting we care about something we were taught not to care about.

Finding the middle ground where we recognize money as a tool that enables options and security rather than as either the measure of our worth or something beneath our notice is work that extends beyond negotiation into general financial wellness. For negotiation purposes, what we need is sufficient clarity to ask for market rates without being paralyzed by shame or guilt, and sufficient detachment to not interpret salary numbers as judgments about our value as humans. This is easier said than achieved, but it's achievable enough that most people can get to functional competence even if we never reach complete emotional neutrality about money.

## The Preparation That Reduces Panic

Preparation for conflict-averse people isn't optional the way it might be for someone who thinks well under pressure and enjoys high-stakes conversations. For us, preparation is the only thing standing between having a coherent negotiation and freezing completely or saying yes just to end the discomfort. The instinct to skip preparation because it forces us to confront the upcoming conversation is strong, but giving in to that instinct guarantees we'll be improvising during the moment when our brain is least capable of forming coherent thoughts. Walking into a salary negotiation without preparation is like trying to give a presentation in a language we barely speak without any notes, technically possible but almost certain to go badly.

The preparation process has to account for what happens to our cognitive function under stress, which means we can't just think about what we want to say, we have to externalize it into documents and scripts we can reference when our working memory stops working. This isn't about memorizing talking points or creating a general outline of themes we want to hit. This is about writing the exact words we'll say, in order, with pauses marked, so when we're sitting in that meeting and our heart is racing and our mind goes blank, we have something concrete to read from rather than trying to compose professional sentences while our amygdala is screaming at us.

Research into market rates is where this starts, and it needs to be specific enough that we can cite it confidently rather than saying vague things about "industry standards" or "what people with my experience typically make." The main sources for salary data are Glassdoor, Levels.fyi, Payscale, Salary.com, and industry-specific surveys that professional associations sometimes publish. Each of these has limitations but together they give us enough information to understand what the real range looks like rather than what we hope it looks like or what employers want us to think it looks like.

Glassdoor aggregates self-reported salary data from employees, which means it's based on what people say they actually make rather than what companies claim they pay. The weakness is that people sometimes inflate their numbers or their data is out of date, and Glassdoor's sample sizes for specific roles at specific companies can be small enough that one or two outliers skew the numbers. The strength is that it's free and covers a huge range of companies and roles, and when there are enough data points, the median numbers are usually reasonably accurate. We want to look at the median rather than the average because averages get pulled up by outliers, and we want to filter by location and years of experience as specifically as possible because salary ranges vary dramatically based on those factors.

Levels.fyi is particularly strong for tech roles because it has very detailed breakdowns of total compensation including base salary, bonuses, stock grants, and signing bonuses for major tech companies. The data comes from employees who submit their offer letters or pay stubs, which means it's generally more reliable than self-reported estimates, and the site shows the progression from entry level through senior roles so we can see what trajectory looks like at different companies. The limitation is that it's primarily tech-focused, so people in other industries need to rely more heavily on other sources, but for anyone negotiating with a software company or a tech-adjacent role, Levels.fyi is probably the single best source of accurate compensation data available publicly.

Payscale and Salary.com use slightly different methodologies, pulling from a combination of self-reported data and employer surveys, and they try to adjust for cost of living and other variables to give more contextualized numbers. The interfaces tend to be clunkier and they often try to upsell premium reports, but the free data is usually sufficient to get a sense of the range. What we're looking for across all these sources is convergence: if three different sites are showing similar numbers for a role, we can be reasonably confident that's close to the actual market rate. If the numbers vary wildly, we need to dig deeper into why and figure out which source is most reliable for our specific situation.

Industry-specific surveys are harder to find but often more accurate than general salary databases because they're tracking narrower populations with more context about what different job titles actually mean. Engineering associations, marketing groups, finance professional organizations, and similar bodies often conduct annual compensation surveys that they publish either publicly or to members. These surveys usually break down by specialization, years of experience, company size, and geography, which gives much more nuanced data than generic job boards. The challenge is finding them, which usually means searching for "[our industry] salary survey 2024" and seeing what comes up, or asking people who are further along in the same field whether they know of reliable sources.

Cost of living adjustments matter more than most people realize because a $90,000 salary in Austin is not financially equivalent to a $90,000 salary in San Francisco or New York. Sites like Numbeo and NerdWallet have cost of living calculators that show the multipliers between different cities, and most salary databases have some version of location adjustment built in, but we need to be careful about how we apply this information in negotiations. If we're negotiating with a company in San Francisco while living in Austin, we don't automatically get San Francisco rates unless we're moving there or the role is explicitly tied to that location's market. Remote work has complicated this calculation because some companies pay based on employee location while others pay based on company headquarters location or some hybrid formula, and there's no universal standard yet.

Company size and funding stage affect compensation in predictable patterns that we need to account for when doing research. Large public companies typically have more rigid salary bands and more established compensation structures, which means the range is narrower but the data is more reliable. Startups have wider variance and often try to make up for lower base salary with equity grants, which may or may not end up being valuable depending on what happens with the company. Mid-size private companies often fall somewhere in between, with more flexibility than enterprises but more structure than early-stage startups. When we're looking at salary data, we need to filter by company size as much as possible because comparing startup offers to Fortune 500 offers without that context will give us misleading expectations.

The 75th percentile of the range is where we want to anchor our negotiation if we're bringing solid relevant experience and can make a strong case for our value. This isn't the top of the range, which is usually reserved for people with exceptional backgrounds or very specialized skills, but it's well above the median, which is where employers typically start their offers. If the range for a role is $70,000 to $110,000 with a median around $85,000, we're aiming for something in the $95,000 to $100,000 range if we have the experience to justify it. This gives us room to come down slightly during negotiation while still landing well above the initial offer, and it signals that we've done research and understand what the market bears rather than just picking a number that sounds good.

The documentation of what we've actually accomplished becomes the evidence we use to justify asking for a number in that range rather than accepting whatever gets offered. This is where most people either do vague hand-waving about "increasing efficiency" and "contributing to team success," or they go too far the other direction and list every task they've ever done regardless of impact. What actually works is identifying three to five specific things we've done that had measurable outcomes, ideally with real numbers attached, and writing them out in a format that connects the action to the result in one or two sentences each.

Examples of what this looks like in practice: "Reduced customer onboarding time from 14 days to 6 days by rebuilding the intake process and eliminating redundant steps, which freed up approximately 160 hours per quarter for the team to focus on higher-value work." Or "Managed the launch of three new product features that collectively generated $400,000 in new revenue in the first six months." Or "Identified a billing error that was costing the company roughly $2,300 per month and worked with finance to implement a fix that recovered those costs going forward." The pattern is action plus specific measurable outcome, not "worked on projects" or "contributed to success."

Getting specific numbers requires going back through old projects and emails and estimates to reconstruct what actually happened, which is time-consuming but necessary because "I think I saved the company a lot of time" doesn't carry any weight in negotiation while "I saved 160 hours per quarter" does. Sometimes the numbers require estimation because we didn't track them precisely at the time, which is fine as long as we're clear about how we arrived at the estimate and the method is reasonable. "Based on processing 40 applications per week at 3 hours each before the change, versus 40 applications at 1.5 hours each after, that's 60 hours saved per week or roughly 240 hours per month" shows our work and makes the claim credible even though we didn't track it to the minute.

For people early in their careers who don't yet have years of accomplishments to draw from, the focus shifts to potential value based on specific skills and relevant experience from internships, coursework, or side projects. "Built a recommendation algorithm for a class project that improved prediction accuracy by 15% compared to the baseline model" demonstrates technical skill even though it wasn't in a job context. "Managed social media accounts for a nonprofit that grew followers from 800 to 3,200 over six months" shows capability around audience growth and content strategy. The numbers might be smaller than what someone ten years into their career can cite, but the principle is the same: specific action, specific measurable outcome.

Writing the actual script means taking the research and the accomplishments and turning them into words we'll say out loud during the negotiation. This isn't a template where we fill in our specific details, this is the exact conversation from start to finish, written out word for word, including the pauses and the parts where we stay quiet and wait for them to respond. The structure that works reliably for first offers looks like this: express genuine enthusiasm for the role and the company, present the specific number we're asking for based on our research, cite one or two key accomplishments that demonstrate we can deliver value at that level, stay silent after stating the number, wait for their response without filling the silence with explanations or justifications or backtracking.

A complete script for responding to a job offer might read: "Thank you for the offer, I'm genuinely excited about this role and about the work the team is doing around [specific project or initiative we learned about during interviews]. Based on my research into market rates for this position, and considering my experience with [specific relevant skill] and my track record around [specific accomplishment with number], I was hoping we could discuss a salary of $95,000. [Pause, say nothing else, wait for them to respond]."

The pause after stating the number is critical because it puts the pressure back on them to respond rather than us continuing to talk and potentially talking ourselves down from what we just asked for. Most of us find silence excruciating and want to fill it with more explanation or softening language like "if that works for you" or "but I'm flexible," and every word we add after the number weakens our position because it signals we're not confident in what we just said. The script needs to explicitly mark where we stop talking, because in the moment our instinct will be to keep going, and overriding that instinct requires having decided in advance that we're going to pause regardless of how uncomfortable it feels.

Some negotiations happen over email rather than in person or on the phone, which changes the dynamic but doesn't change the need for scripted language. Email negotiation has the advantage that we can write and revise without time pressure, but it has the disadvantage that tone is harder to convey and it's easier for employers to delay or avoid the conversation by just not responding quickly. The script for email negotiation uses the same structure as the verbal script but needs to be slightly more detailed because we don't have the back-and-forth of conversation to clarify things. We still express enthusiasm, cite research and accomplishments, state our number, and avoid hedging language, but we might add one sentence about our flexibility around other components of the compensation package if salary is constrained.

Writing down our minimum acceptable number before the conversation starts is a separate but related part of preparation. This is the number below which we walk away or at least take significant time to think rather than accepting in the moment. It needs to be written down physically, not just thought about, because once we're in the negotiation our anxiety will make us want to accept less than we planned, and having the line on paper gives us something concrete to reference. The minimum should be based on the research we did about the low end of the reasonable range plus our own financial needs and risk tolerance, not on what we hope they'll offer or what would make us happy. It's the floor, not the target.

Deciding the minimum in advance also prevents us from having to make that judgment call in real time when we're already stressed and our thinking is compromised. If they come back with $82,000 and our minimum is $85,000, we know immediately that we need to counter again or explore other compensation components rather than trying to decide in the moment whether $82,000 is close enough to what we wanted. The minimum isn't necessarily something we share with the employer, it's our internal boundary that we commit to respecting regardless of how much we want the conversation to be over.

Practicing the script out loud, multiple times, is what moves it from words on a page to something we can actually execute when our voice wants to shake and our brain wants to shut down. Reading silently doesn't prepare us for how the words feel coming out of our mouth or how long the pauses actually are or where we naturally want to rush through parts that feel uncomfortable. We need to say the words, hear ourselves saying them, adjust phrasing that sounds awkward when spoken even though it reads fine, and get comfortable with the pauses that feel endless when we're doing them live but are actually only three or four seconds.

Recording ourselves practicing can be useful if we can stand to listen back to it, because we often don't notice verbal tics or filler words or pace issues when we're just running through it in our head. Hearing "um" or "like" or nervous laughter that we're not aware we do gives us something specific to work on eliminating before the real conversation. Practicing with another person who can play the employer role is even better if we have someone we trust enough to do this with, because it introduces the dynamic of responding to another human rather than just reciting to ourselves, and they can give feedback about tone or phrasing that might land differently than we intended.

The practice sessions don't need to be elaborate or formal, they just need to happen enough times that the script starts to feel somewhat familiar rather than completely foreign. Three to five run-throughs is usually enough to get comfortable with the basic flow without over-rehearsing to the point where it sounds robotic. We're not trying to memorize it perfectly, we're trying to build enough familiarity that when we're stressed and can't remember the exact wording, we can still hit the main points in approximately the right order.

For people who think better on their feet and find scripts constraining, the alternative is to prepare a framework rather than exact language, but this only works if our anxiety doesn't completely shut down our ability to think during the conversation. The framework version means knowing the key points we need to make: express interest, cite research, state our number, reference specific value we bring, stay quiet after the number. We improvise the exact words but we have the structure to guide us. Most conflict-averse people can't reliably do this because the stress response interferes too much with real-time composure, which is why the scripted version works better for us even though it feels more rigid.

Introverts have specific advantages in the preparation phase that we can lean into rather than treating our tendencies as weaknesses. We're generally better at deep research and sustained focus than extroverts who get bored with that kind of detailed work. We're better at thinking through scenarios in advance and anticipating different directions the conversation might go. We're better at written communication, which means if we can negotiate by email we're often more articulate there than we are in live conversation. These aren't personality flaws to overcome, they're natural strengths that make certain parts of negotiation easier for us if we structure the process to play to them.

The time investment for proper preparation is somewhere between four and eight hours total, spread across research, documentation, script writing, and practice. This feels like a lot when we're already anxious about the upcoming conversation and would rather not think about it at all, but it's also insurance against the alternative, which is winging it and accepting whatever gets offered because we didn't give ourselves the tools to do anything else. Four hours of uncomfortable preparation work versus potentially losing $300,000 over a career is not a difficult calculation once we frame it that way, even though in the moment the four hours feels more real than the theoretical future money.

Breaking the preparation into smaller chunks makes it less overwhelming than trying to do everything in one session. Day one can be just research, collecting salary data from three different sources and writing down the ranges we find. Day two can be documenting our accomplishments, going through old projects and pulling out the specific numbers. Day three can be writing the script, using the research and accomplishments to construct the exact words we'll say. Day four can be practice runs, saying the script out loud at least three times. This spreads the discomfort across multiple days rather than requiring us to sit with it for hours at once, which makes it more manageable for people who find the topic depleting.

Some of us procrastinate on preparation because engaging with it makes the negotiation feel more real and therefore more threatening, which is understandable but ultimately counterproductive. The negotiation is happening regardless of whether we prepare for it, and avoiding preparation doesn't make it less scary, it just makes it more likely to go badly. Naming the avoidance as a fear response rather than a time management issue helps because it clarifies what we're actually dealing with, which is not "I don't have time to prepare" but "thinking about this makes me anxious so I'm avoiding it even though I know avoidance will make the outcome worse."

The preparation we're describing here is front-loaded work that pays off in every future negotiation, not just the immediate one we're facing. Once we have a salary research process that works, we can replicate it for future job searches in a fraction of the time. Once we have a script template that we've used successfully, we can adapt it for raises or new offers without starting from scratch. Once we've practiced negotiating and survived the conversation, the second time is less terrifying than the first even though it doesn't become comfortable. The skills and systems compound the same way the money does, and the initial time investment creates infrastructure we'll use repeatedly over decades.

# The Exact Words to Say

Scripts work for anxious negotiators because they remove the need to compose sentences under stress, which is when our brain is least capable of doing that work well. What follows are the actual words to use in common scenarios, written to be copied directly rather than adapted or personalized. These aren't templates with blanks to fill in, they're complete conversations that account for the back-and-forth that happens during real negotiations and include guidance about where to pause, where to stay silent, and what the other person is likely to say in response.

The structure of every successful script follows the same basic pattern regardless of the specific situation: express genuine interest or appreciation first so we're not leading with demands, present our request with specific reasoning based on research or accomplishments, state the number or ask for the specific thing we want, then stop talking and wait for their response. The instinct to keep explaining or justifying after we've made our request is almost universal among conflict-averse people, and it undermines everything that came before it because continued talking signals uncertainty about what we just said. The pause after our request is where most negotiations are won or lost, which is why the scripts explicitly mark where to be quiet.

When the initial offer is lower than expected and we need to counter, the script starts with acknowledgment that we received the offer and genuine enthusiasm about the opportunity, because people are more willing to negotiate with candidates who clearly want the job than with people who seem to be using them as leverage for other offers. The enthusiasm needs to be authentic rather than performed, which means we only use this script if we actually do want the job. If we're ambivalent or just fishing for higher numbers to take back to another employer, that comes across in tone and body language regardless of the words we say.

The complete script for responding to a first offer that's too low: "Thank you for the offer, I'm genuinely excited about this role and about what the team is building, particularly around [specific project or initiative that came up during interviews and that we actually care about]. I've done research on market rates for this position, and given my experience with [specific skill that's relevant to the job] and my track record around [specific accomplishment with a number attached], I was thinking something in the range of [target salary number]. Is there room to move on the salary?"

The pause after "Is there room to move on the salary?" is critical. We say nothing else. We don't add "if that works for your budget" or "but I'm flexible" or "I understand if that's not possible." We ask the question and then we sit in the silence while they think about their response. This silence will feel like it lasts five minutes when it's actually fifteen seconds, and every instinct we have will be screaming at us to fill it with more words. We don't fill it. We wait.

What they say next typically falls into one of four categories. They might say some version of "let me see what I can do" or "I need to check with my manager," which means the negotiation is working and we stay in the conversation without conceding anything yet. They might immediately counter with a number that's between their first offer and our request, which means we evaluate whether that's acceptable or whether we push for more. They might say "that's outside our range for this role," which doesn't mean no, it means we need to either justify the higher number more clearly or shift to discussing other components of compensation. Or they might, rarely, just agree to our number, which happens more often than anxious negotiators expect because many hiring managers have flexibility they don't advertise and they respect candidates who know their worth.

If they come back with "let me see what I can do," our response is simply "I appreciate that, take the time you need." We don't apologize for asking, we don't walk back our number, we just acknowledge that they need to go through their process. If they say "I need to talk to my manager," the same response works. This is actually a positive sign because it means they're advocating for us internally rather than just rejecting our request outright, but our anxiety will interpret it as a bad sign because we're not getting immediate acceptance. Recognizing this interpretation bias helps us avoid sabotaging ourselves by lowering our ask while they're in the middle of trying to get us more money.

If they counter with a number that's between their original offer and our request, we need to decide in the moment whether to accept it, push for more, or explore other compensation components. This decision is easier if we wrote down our minimum acceptable number before the conversation started, because then we're just comparing their counter to our predetermined floor rather than trying to calculate what's reasonable while stressed. If their counter is above our minimum and close to our target, we can accept it with "That works for me, thank you." If it's below our minimum, we say "I appreciate you moving on this. Given the research I did on market rates and the value I know I can bring, could we get to [number that's halfway between their counter and our original request]?"

The reason we meet them halfway in the second counter rather than holding firm at our original number is that negotiation requires some give and take, and being completely inflexible reads as unreasonable rather than confident. We're showing that we heard their constraints while still advocating for compensation that reflects our value. If they still can't meet us at the halfway point, that's when we shift to asking about other components of the package rather than continuing to push on base salary alone.

When they say "that's outside our range for this role," many people hear this as a hard no and immediately back down. What it actually means is either they genuinely can't pay that much for this level position, or they need more justification for why we're worth more than the typical range. Our response: "I understand there's a range for the role. What I'm bringing is [specific skill or experience that's above what they typically see in candidates], and based on [specific accomplishment with numbers], I've demonstrated I can deliver [specific value that matters to their business]. Given that, does [our target number] work?"

This response reframes the conversation from "you're asking for too much" to "here's why I'm worth more than the typical candidate for this position." We're not arguing with their range, we're making the case that we should be at the top of it or slightly above it because of specific capabilities they need. If they still say it's not possible, we move to the comprehensive compensation discussion: "I hear you on the salary constraints. What about the total package? I'm thinking about signing bonus, additional PTO, professional development budget, stock options, or remote work flexibility. Where might we find some room?"

The signing bonus conversation is valuable because it's one-time money that doesn't affect the ongoing salary budget the way a higher base would, which means hiring managers often have more flexibility here than they admit initially. If we're $7,000 apart on base salary and they truly can't move, a $7,000 signing bonus partially closes that gap, and while it doesn't compound the way salary does, it's real money that changes the financial picture of accepting the offer. The script for asking about signing bonus: "If the base salary is truly fixed at [their number], would a signing bonus be possible to help close the gap? I was thinking something in the range of [amount that's roughly equal to our salary gap]."

Professional development budget is another component that many companies overlook in initial offers but have budget for if we ask. This might be $2,000 to $5,000 per year for conferences, courses, certifications, or books, and while it's not cash in hand, it has real value for our long-term earning potential because it keeps our skills current and our network growing. The script: "Does the company offer a professional development budget? I'm interested in staying current with [specific area relevant to the job], and having a budget for courses and conferences would be valuable."

Additional PTO is worth real money when we calculate it based on our daily rate, and many companies have some flexibility here even when they claim their PTO policy is standard. An extra week of vacation for someone making $80,000 is worth roughly $1,540 in annual compensation. Two extra weeks is worth $3,080. The script for negotiating PTO: "The salary works for me. On the PTO side, I'm currently at [current number] weeks, would it be possible to start with [one or two weeks more than their standard policy]?"

Stock options or equity grants are standard at startups and tech companies but possible at other companies if we ask, and they represent potentially significant value even though they're risky and illiquid in the short term. The script for asking about equity: "I'm excited about the company's growth trajectory. Is equity part of the compensation package for this role? I'd be interested in discussing an options grant as part of the offer."

Remote work flexibility has become a major negotiation point since 2020, and companies vary wildly in how much flexibility they offer. If the role is advertised as hybrid or in-office and we want full remote, the negotiation is harder than if they're already offering hybrid and we want to optimize the terms. The script for negotiating remote work: "On the remote work policy, is there flexibility in the schedule? I'm most productive when I can work from home [specific number] days per week, would that be possible for this role?"

The conversation about remote work needs to account for what we've learned about the company culture during interviews. If they've emphasized in-person collaboration and team building, asking for full remote might signal we're not aligned with their values, which could hurt our chances more than it helps. If they've already said the role is hybrid, asking for one additional remote day per week is usually reasonable. Reading the room matters here more than in pure compensation discussions because remote work touches on culture and management philosophy in ways that salary doesn't.

Performance review timing is something almost nobody negotiates but that has real financial impact because earlier reviews mean earlier raises. Standard practice at many companies is annual reviews at the end of the calendar year or on work anniversaries, but we can sometimes negotiate a six-month review instead of waiting a full year for our first raise. The script: "On the review cycle, I'd like to propose a six-month initial review rather than waiting a full year, so we can evaluate fit and performance sooner and adjust compensation if warranted. Does that work?"

This framing works because it positions the early review as benefiting both sides rather than just being a way for us to get a raise faster. Companies actually do want to know within six months whether a new hire is working out, and attaching a compensation review to that checkpoint is reasonable. Not every company will agree, but asking costs nothing and occasionally results in an earlier path to higher pay.

When we're negotiating a raise with our current employer rather than responding to a job offer, the script structure shifts because the power dynamic is different. We don't have the leverage of walking away that we do with external offers, and we're asking someone we have an ongoing relationship with rather than a hiring manager we just met. The preparation for an internal raise negotiation requires more documentation of accomplishments because the burden of proof is higher when we're asking for an exception to the standard raise cycle.

The complete script for requesting a raise: "I wanted to talk about my compensation. Over the past [timeframe, usually 12 to 18 months], I've [first major accomplishment with specific numbers], I've also [second major accomplishment with specific numbers], and I took on [additional responsibility that wasn't part of the original role]. Based on my research into market rates for someone with my experience doing this work, and based on the value I've been delivering, I'd like to discuss moving my salary to [specific number that represents 10 to 20 percent increase]. What would it take to make that happen?"

The ending question "what would it take to make that happen" is deliberately open-ended because internal raise discussions often involve processes and timelines and budget cycles that we might not be aware of as employees. We're not demanding an immediate decision, we're opening a conversation about what the path looks like. This gives our manager room to explain constraints without saying no outright, and it positions us as someone who understands business realities rather than someone who's making entitled demands.

Our manager's response will likely be some version of "I need to talk to HR" or "we do raises in December" or "I'll see what I can do but budget is tight this year." Our follow-up depends on what they say. If they need to check with HR, we say "I understand, what's the timeline for getting back to me on this?" If they mention the standard raise cycle, we say "I'm aware of the December cycle, I'm asking about an off-cycle adjustment given [brief restatement of our value add]." If they cite budget constraints, we say "I understand budget is tight, what about adjusting my title or expanding my professional development budget as interim steps?"

The title adjustment conversation is worth having separately from pure compensation because titles affect our market value when we eventually change jobs even if they don't change our paycheck immediately. Moving from Associate to Senior Associate or from Analyst to Manager costs the company nothing in the short term but makes us more marketable externally, which gives us leverage in future negotiations. The script for negotiating title: "Given the responsibilities I've taken on around [specific responsibility that typically belongs to the next level], would it make sense to adjust my title to [next title up]? I'm thinking about how this role is positioned for internal growth and for how it translates externally."

When our manager says no to our raise request, most of us accept that as final and drop the conversation, but the first no is rarely the end of the discussion unless we make it the end by giving up. The script for responding to an initial no: "I appreciate you being direct about that. Can you help me understand what would need to change for this to be possible? Is it timing, is it about hitting specific metrics, is it budget, or is it something else?"

This question forces specificity about why we're being told no, which either gives us a concrete path forward or reveals that the no isn't actually about our performance or value but about company constraints we can't control. If they say we need to wait until the next review cycle, we ask what metrics or accomplishments would justify the increase we're requesting at that review. If they say budget is frozen, we ask when budget might open up and what we should be documenting in the meantime. If they say our performance needs to improve, we ask for specific examples of what improvement looks like so we have clear targets.

The goal in responding to no is to turn it from a conversation-ender into information we can use to either change the outcome or make an informed decision about whether staying makes sense. If our manager can't articulate what would need to be different for them to approve our raise request, that's actually valuable information because it suggests the no isn't about anything we can control through better performance.

When we're told that salary is completely fixed with no room to negotiate, which happens primarily with government jobs, large companies with rigid bands, or positions where the compensation is set by union contracts or formal pay scales, we still have the conversation about other components but we adjust our expectations. The script for this situation: "I understand the salary is non-negotiable. Let's talk about the rest of the package. I'm interested in discussing [list two or three things that matter most to us: PTO, remote work, professional development, start date, moving assistance, title]."

Even in rigid systems, there's usually flexibility somewhere if we know where to look for it. Government jobs often have steps within grades that allow for some movement based on experience. Union positions sometimes have different classifications that come with different pay levels. Large companies have more room on signing bonuses and stock grants than they do on base salary. The key is not assuming that "salary is fixed" means "nothing is negotiable."

The start date can be a negotiation point that people overlook because it doesn't seem like it's about money, but delaying our start date by two or four weeks when we're transitioning between jobs gives us time to rest and handle personal business without burning PTO from the new job immediately. The script: "On the start date, would it be possible to start on [date that's two weeks later than they proposed]? I'd like to take a short break between roles to handle some personal matters."

Moving assistance is standard for relocations but the amount varies, and if we're moving across the country for a job, asking for $5,000 or $10,000 to cover expenses is reasonable even if they didn't mention it in the initial offer. The script: "Since this involves relocating from [current city] to [new city], I wanted to ask about moving assistance. Would the company be able to provide [specific dollar amount] to cover moving costs?"

When someone pressures us to make a decision immediately, either on a job offer or on accepting their counter-offer without further negotiation, the script is simple but requires us to hold firm against the social pressure: "I need 24 hours to review everything and make sure I'm thinking clearly about the full package. I'll get back to you tomorrow by [specific time]."

The time request works even when they say they need an answer today because most urgent deadlines in hiring are artificial or flexible. If they genuinely rescind an offer because we asked for one day to think about it, that's information about what it would be like to work there, and we've probably dodged a bad situation. In almost all cases, they'll agree to the delay because they want us to feel good about accepting, and accepting under time pressure doesn't create that feeling.

When we're asking for a specific benefit rather than salary, the framing matters because we're acknowledging it might be unusual while still presenting it as a reasonable request. The script for unusual requests: "One thing that would make a real difference for me is [specific thing: four-day work week, unlimited PTO, sabbatical policy, working from another country for part of the year]. I know this might not be standard, but is it something we could include in my offer?"

The "I know this might not be standard" phrasing gives them room to say no without it being awkward, but it also plants the seed that we're someone who thinks creatively about compensation beyond just salary, which sometimes leads to them proposing alternatives we wouldn't have thought to ask for.

Email negotiation uses the same content as verbal negotiation but needs slightly different phrasing because we don't have tone of voice and body language to convey enthusiasm and seriousness. The email version needs to be more explicit about both our interest in the role and our reasoning for the request. A complete email negotiation looks like this:

"Hi [Hiring Manager],

Thank you so much for the offer to join [Company] as [Job Title]. I'm genuinely excited about the opportunity to work on [specific project or team focus that we discussed in interviews and actually care about], and I think there's strong alignment between what the team needs and what I bring.

I've been thinking about the compensation package, and I wanted to discuss the base salary. I did research on market rates for this role using [we can mention Glassdoor, Payscale, or industry sources, but don't need to list all of them], and given my experience with [specific relevant skill] and my track record around [specific accomplishment with numbers], I was hoping we could land at [specific target number].

I'm very interested in moving forward, and I'm confident I can deliver significant value in this role. Let me know if there's flexibility on the salary, or if there are other components of the package we should discuss.

Looking forward to hearing from you, [Our name]"

This email does several things: it confirms we want the job, it presents research-backed reasoning for our number, it cites specific value we bring, it states our target clearly, and it leaves room for them to either agree or propose alternatives. The tone stays collaborative rather than adversarial, which matters more in email than in person because there's no opportunity to course-correct if we come across wrong.

When they respond to our email with their counter or with questions, we continue the same pattern: acknowledge their response, address their questions or concerns, restate our position with additional justification if needed, and keep the door open for continued conversation. Email negotiations often take several rounds of back-and-forth that happen over days rather than in one sitting, which actually works in our favor as conflict-averse negotiators because we can compose our responses carefully rather than reacting in real time.

The final acceptance email after successful negotiation should be warm and professional without reopening any of the negotiated points. Once we've agreed to terms, we don't add "I'm so glad we could work that out" or "thank you for being flexible" because that language implies they did us a favor rather than that we negotiated to fair market rates. The acceptance email: "Hi [Hiring Manager], I'm excited to accept the offer and join the team. Looking forward to starting on [date]. Please send over the formal offer letter when you have it ready."

These scripts work because they're specific enough to use verbatim but flexible enough to adapt to different industries and contexts. The exact dollar amounts change, the specific accomplishments we cite change, the benefits we prioritize change, but the structure and phrasing stay consistent. We're always expressing genuine interest, presenting research-backed requests, citing specific value we bring, making clear asks, and leaving space for conversation rather than ultimatums.

What makes these scripts effective for anxious negotiators specifically is that they remove the improvisation burden during moments of high stress, they explicitly mark where to be silent instead of talking ourselves down, and they frame everything as business conversation rather than personal confrontation. We're not asking for favors, we're not apologizing for having standards, we're not performing confidence we don't feel. We're stating what we know about market rates, what we've accomplished, and what we're looking for, and then we're waiting to see if the other side can meet us there.

The scripts for handling specific objections or pushback require more nuance because the employer is testing whether we're serious about our number or whether we'll fold if they apply pressure. When they say "that's significantly higher than what we budgeted for this role," we need to distinguish between genuine budget constraints and negotiating tactics. Our response: "I understand budget considerations are real. The number I mentioned is based on market research for someone with my background doing this specific work. If [our target number] genuinely doesn't work, can you share what you had budgeted so we can talk about whether we can close the gap?"

This response does two things: it validates that budgets are real constraints without immediately accepting that their budget is reasonable, and it asks them to share their number, which gives us information we didn't have before. Many hiring managers won't share the budgeted range, but some will, and knowing where they started their thinking helps us understand how far apart we actually are versus how far apart they're claiming we are.

When they say "we've never paid someone at your level this much before," that's actually information that works in our favor because it confirms we're asking for something at the top of their range rather than something completely unreasonable. Our response: "I appreciate you being transparent about that. What I'm hearing is that [our number] would be at the high end of what you've paid for this role. Given [specific skill or accomplishment that differentiates us from typical candidates], I think there's a strong case for being at that high end. Does that make sense?"

The framing here acknowledges their concern while making the case that we're not a typical candidate so their typical pay range might not apply. We're not arguing that they're wrong about their historical patterns, we're arguing that we're an exception worth making for those patterns.

When they try to sell us on "opportunity" or "growth potential" instead of higher pay, we need to acknowledge the opportunity is real while still anchoring on current market rates. The script: "I'm definitely excited about the growth opportunity here, and that's a big part of why I'm interested in the role. At the same time, I need the base compensation to reflect current market rates for what I'm bringing to the team. The opportunity and the fair compensation aren't mutually exclusive, so let's figure out how to make both work."

This response refuses the frame that we should accept lower pay in exchange for future potential, which is a trade most people regret because future potential often doesn't materialize the way employers suggest it will. We're saying we want both fair current pay and good future prospects, which is perfectly reasonable even though employers sometimes present them as either-or choices.

When they mention equity or stock options as if that compensates for lower base salary, we acknowledge the equity while insisting on market-rate base pay. The script: "I appreciate that equity is part of the package, and I'm optimistic about the company's trajectory. Equity is inherently risky and illiquid, though, so I'm focused on getting the base salary to market rate first, and then equity is an additional upside on top of that rather than a substitute for fair base pay."

This framing is important because many startups try to sell candidates on equity as if it's equivalent to cash, when actually equity in private companies is highly speculative and can't be used to pay rent or student loans. We're not refusing equity, we're refusing to accept lower cash compensation in exchange for it.

When they say "this is really our final offer," we need to test whether that's actually true or whether it's a negotiating position. The script: "I appreciate you being direct. Before I make a final decision, let me make sure I understand the full picture. The base salary is [their number], and that's truly fixed with no room to move. What about [list two or three other components: signing bonus, stock, PTO, title, review timeline]? Is there flexibility in any of those areas?"

Many times what they mean by final offer is "final offer on base salary" but they have flexibility elsewhere, and if we accept the "final offer" framing without testing other components, we leave value on the table. If they say everything is truly fixed with no flexibility anywhere, we're in a take-it-or-leave-it situation, but that's actually rare, and it's worth confirming before we accept it.

The script for when we have competing offers is delicate because we don't want to make it sound like we're playing companies against each other, which can backfire. The phrasing: "I wanted to be transparent that I'm also considering another offer, and that offer is at [competing offer amount or description of compensation package]. I'm more excited about this role because of [specific reasons related to work, team, or mission], but I need to make a decision that makes sense financially as well. Is there room to adjust the compensation so I can move forward here?"

This script is honest about the competing offer without using it as a threat, and it emphasizes that we prefer their company for substantive reasons rather than just whoever pays most. The risk with mentioning competing offers is that some employers will decide we're not seriously interested and withdraw, while others will use it as motivation to increase their offer. We only use this script if we genuinely do prefer their role and would take it if the compensation were closer to the competing offer.

When discussing salary in states where it's illegal to ask about previous compensation, we need to be prepared for employers who ask anyway, either because they're unaware of the law or because they're testing whether we know our rights. The script: "I'm not comfortable sharing my current salary, and I understand in [state name] it's not a permitted question. I'm happy to discuss what this role is worth based on market data and what I bring to it."

This response is firm without being confrontational. We're not accusing them of illegal behavior, we're just declining to answer and refocusing on the relevant information. If they push after this, that's a red flag about whether they respect legal boundaries and candidate rights.

When we're negotiating and they seem offended or surprised that we're negotiating at all, which happens more often to women than to men, we need to reframe the conversation as normal business practice. The script: "I see this as a standard business conversation about ensuring the compensation reflects market rates and the value I bring. I'm absolutely still very interested in the role, and I want to start from a place that works for both of us long-term."

This script does several things: it normalizes the negotiation as business rather than personal, it reaffirms our interest so they don't think we're being difficult for the sake of it, and it frames fair compensation as something that benefits them too because underpaid employees become resentful and leave. The tone needs to stay calm and professional rather than defensive, which is hard when we're feeling judged for negotiating, but defensiveness will confirm their worst assumptions while calm professionalism often shifts their perception.

The script for negotiating when we're changing industries or taking a role that's somewhat different from our previous experience requires acknowledging the transition while still anchoring on our skills and results. The example: "I know I'm transitioning from [previous industry] to [new industry], and I understand that means some learning curve. What I'm bringing is [transferable skill], [another transferable skill], and a track record of [specific type of results that's relevant across industries]. Based on research into what people with similar skill sets make in this market, I'm looking at [target number]."

This framing prevents them from anchoring our salary to what we made in our previous industry if that industry typically paid less, while also acknowledging the transition is real. We're not claiming to be worth exactly what someone who's been in their industry for ten years would make, but we're also not accepting that our previous industry salary is the ceiling.

When negotiating compensation for a promotion within our current company, we face different dynamics because they know exactly what we're making now and they have established internal equity concerns about keeping pay fair across team members. The script: "I'm excited about the opportunity to move into [new role]. Given the increased scope and responsibilities, I wanted to discuss the compensation. This role typically has a salary range of [research-based range], and given my knowledge of the team and our work, I'd like to discuss landing at [number in the 75th percentile of that range]. What would it take to make that happen?"

The "what would it take" framing is particularly useful for internal promotions because it acknowledges there might be processes or constraints we're not aware of while still making clear we expect meaningful compensation increase for meaningful responsibility increase. We're not just asking "can I have more money," we're asking "what's the path to appropriate compensation for this level."

When we're negotiating as someone returning to work after a career break, whether for parenting, caregiving, health reasons, or anything else, we face potential discrimination around the gap and around whether we're still worth market rates. The script: "I took [timeframe] off to [brief reason, without over-explaining], and I'm excited to be returning to work in this field. During that time I [any relevant skill maintenance: took courses, did consulting projects, stayed current with industry developments]. Based on my total experience and what people with my background typically make in the current market, I'm looking at [target salary]."

This script acknowledges the gap without being apologetic about it, provides brief context for those who need it to feel comfortable, demonstrates we stayed engaged with the field if that's true, and anchors firmly on current market rates rather than on what we made before the break. The tendency is to accept lower offers after career breaks because we're grateful someone hired us, but that gratitude costs us real money over the remainder of our career.

The negotiation for contract or consulting roles follows different patterns than employment because we're negotiating both rate and terms, and the relationship is explicitly transactional rather than relationship-based in the same way employment is. The script for hourly rate: "My rate for this type of work is [hourly rate based on market research]. For a project of this scope, I estimate [total hours], which would come to [total project cost]. Does that work within your budget?"

If they push back on our hourly rate, we can discuss project-based pricing instead, which takes the focus off our hourly rate and puts it on the total value they're getting: "If hourly pricing doesn't work, I could propose a flat project fee of [amount] to deliver [specific deliverables by specific date]. That gives you cost certainty and takes the hourly tracking out of the equation."

Contract work also involves negotiating payment terms, which employment doesn't, and this matters for cash flow and for signaling whether the client respects our work. The script for payment terms: "On payment terms, I require [50% upfront before starting work, or 30% upfront with 30% at midpoint and 40% on completion, or whatever structure we prefer]. For projects over [dollar amount], I invoice every two weeks for completed work with payment due within 15 days."

The upfront payment request protects us from clients who disappear or decide they don't want to pay after we've done the work, and clients who are serious about the project won't balk at reasonable deposit requirements. If they refuse any upfront payment, that's often a red flag about whether they'll actually pay when the work is complete.

Negotiating as someone relatively early in career without extensive accomplishments to point to requires different evidence than what more experienced people use, but the structure stays similar. The script: "I know I'm early in my career, but I want to talk about what I'm bringing that's relevant to this role. I have [specific technical skill at high proficiency level], I demonstrated [specific capability through project or internship with measurable outcome], and I learn new systems quickly, which I showed by [specific example of picking something up fast]. Based on market research for entry-level people with this skill set in this location, I'm looking at [target salary in the upper range for entry level]."

This script doesn't pretend we have ten years of experience, but it also doesn't apologize for being early career. We're stating what we do bring and asking for compensation that reflects that value at the appropriate level. Early career negotiations are still worth having even though the dollar amounts involved are smaller, because they set trajectory just like mid-career negotiations do.

The script for negotiating when we're being recruited away from a job we like requires balancing genuine interest in the new opportunity with attachment to where we are, and we can use that attachment as leverage without being dishonest. The example: "I'm definitely intrigued by this role, especially because of [specific aspect of their work that appeals to us]. I should be clear though that I'm happy where I am, so for me to move, the opportunity needs to be compelling both in terms of the work and in terms of compensation. I've done research on what this role typically pays, and to make a move worthwhile, I'd need to be at [number that's at or above the top of the market range]."

This framing is honest about the fact that they need to beat our current situation significantly to get us to leave, which gives us more leverage than if we seemed desperate for any new job. We're not bluffing or playing games, we're accurately describing our situation, and that situation genuinely does mean they need to offer more to move us.

When salary discussions are happening over multiple conversations rather than all at once, we need to keep track of what's been agreed to and what's still open. After each conversation, we send a brief email summarizing what we understand to have been decided: "Thanks for the conversation today. Just to confirm my understanding: base salary of [amount], starting [date], with [other confirmed details]. We're still discussing [things that remain open]. Looking forward to continuing the conversation."

This email serves two purposes: it prevents misunderstandings where we thought they agreed to something and they thought we were just discussing possibilities, and it documents the negotiation process in writing so there's a record if disagreements emerge later. The tone stays professional and collaborative rather than legalistic, but the content creates clarity about what's been settled.

Throughout all of these scenarios, the underlying principle stays consistent: we're having business conversations about market rates and value exchange, we're being specific about what we want and why, we're giving the other party room to work with us on finding solutions, and we're refusing to accept the first no as final. The exact words vary by situation but the approach of preparation, clarity, silence after requests, and persistence through initial objections applies universally to every negotiation context we'll encounter over a career.

# Managing the Moment When We Want to Run

Preparation and scripts give us the content for negotiation but they don't eliminate the physical panic that shows up when we're actually in the conversation trying to execute what we planned. Our voice shakes, our face gets hot, our mind goes blank, and every cell in our body is screaming to just agree to whatever they're offering so we can end this and escape. These physical responses happen even when we've prepared thoroughly because preparation addresses the cognitive challenge while the panic is physiological, and managing it requires different tools than having the right words to say.

The voice shaking is often the first thing we notice because it's audible to the other person in a way our racing heart isn't, and the awareness that they can hear our nervousness creates a secondary wave of anxiety that makes the shaking worse. The physical mechanism is that stress tightens the muscles around our vocal cords and makes precise control harder, which is why our pitch wobbles or our volume becomes inconsistent or we hear ourselves sounding breathy when we're trying to sound confident. Trying to force steadiness through willpower doesn't work because we can't consciously control those muscles when they're already in a stress response.

What does work is accepting the shake rather than fighting it. When we notice our voice trembling during a negotiation, we can acknowledge it directly with something like "I get nervous having these conversations, but I mean what I'm saying" and then continue with whatever we were saying as if the acknowledgment was just a minor aside rather than a major derailment. This takes the power out of the symptom by naming it before the other person has time to wonder about it, and it reframes nervousness as a normal human response rather than a sign of inadequacy. Most hiring managers and bosses have experienced nervousness themselves at some point and respond to honest acknowledgment better than they respond to obvious attempts to hide what's clearly happening.

The alternative approach if acknowledging the shake directly feels too vulnerable is to simply slow down our speech deliberately. Slower speech gives us more control over our voice and makes any tremor less noticeable because we're not rushing through words. The instinct under stress is to talk faster to get the uncomfortable moment over with, but faster speech amplifies any vocal instability while slower speech dampens it. We can practice this by speaking our negotiation script at half our normal pace when we're preparing, which feels absurdly slow when we're calm but will feel approximately normal when we're actually negotiating and our body wants us to rush.

The mind-going-blank problem shows up as that terrifying moment when we know we had something specific to say and we can't retrieve it, like the information exists somewhere in our brain but the stress has temporarily locked the door to that room. This is cortisol interfering with working memory and retrieval processes, and it's not a sign that we didn't prepare enough or that we're not smart enough to negotiate, it's just what stress does to human brains regardless of intelligence or preparation quality. The solution is externalizing the information we need so we're not relying on memory retrieval under stress.

Having our script written on paper or on our laptop in front of us during the negotiation means when our mind blanks we can just read what we wrote when we were thinking clearly. This feels like cheating somehow, as if we're supposed to negotiate entirely from memory to prove we're competent, but that's self-sabotage based on an arbitrary standard we invented. Lawyers reference notes during trials, surgeons reference protocols during procedures, pilots reference checklists during flights, and somehow we've decided we need to negotiate life-changing compensation without any external support. We can let go of that standard and just read from our notes when we need to, which turns a moment of panic into a minor pause where we glance at our paper and then continue.

The specific technique for using notes without it looking like we're completely lost is to pause when we feel ourselves blanking, say "let me make sure I'm covering everything," look at our notes, find our place, and then continue from there. The pause and the explicit acknowledgment that we're checking our notes prevents the awkward moment where we're obviously reading but pretending we're not, which is what actually makes people uncomfortable. If we're transparent about referencing notes, it comes across as thorough preparation rather than inadequacy.

Silence after we state our number or make our request is where most negotiations are won or lost, and it's also where our discomfort peaks because we're sitting in uncertainty while they think about their response. The silence feels like it lasts five minutes when it's actually fifteen to thirty seconds, and the urge to fill it with more words is almost overwhelming. We want to add softening language like "if that works for you" or justifications like "I know that's high but" or escape clauses like "but I'm flexible," and every one of these additions weakens our position by signaling we don't actually believe in what we just said.

Staying silent requires actively stopping ourselves from talking, which is harder than it sounds when anxiety is telling us that silence is dangerous and we need to fix it immediately. The technique is to close our mouth physically, even clench our teeth if necessary, and count slowly to ten in our head while maintaining eye contact or neutral body language. If we get to ten and they still haven't responded, we can count to ten again. At some point they will say something because silence is uncomfortable for them too, and whoever speaks first after a request has been made is at a disadvantage in negotiation because they're either accepting the request or rejecting it or proposing an alternative, all of which gives us information and keeps the ball in play.

The specific sensation that silence creates for anxious people is a kind of social pain that registers similarly to physical pain in brain imaging studies. We're not being dramatic when we say silence feels unbearable, it actually activates pain processing regions in the brain, which is why the urge to end it is so strong. Knowing this doesn't make silence comfortable but it does help us understand that the intensity of discomfort we feel isn't a sign we're doing something wrong, it's just our brain processing social uncertainty as threatening.

When we're negotiating over video call rather than in person, the silence becomes even more awkward because we can see our own face on screen in addition to theirs, and we become hyperaware of our expression and how we're coming across. The temptation to fill the silence is stronger because video calls already feel more stilted than in-person conversation. The solution is to turn off self-view so we're not watching ourselves during the negotiation, which removes one source of self-consciousness and makes it easier to focus on what they're saying rather than how we look saying it.

Phone negotiations without video remove the visual awkwardness but create different challenges because we can't see their facial expressions or body language to gauge how they're receiving our request. This uncertainty often makes us talk more than we should because we're trying to compensate for the missing visual feedback. The technique for phone negotiation is having our script and notes in front of us even more explicitly than we would in person, because we can reference them freely without anyone seeing us do it, which actually makes phone negotiation easier for people who rely heavily on preparation.

The heat rising in our face and neck that happens during stressful moments is blood flow changes related to the fight-or-flight response, and it's visible enough that other people can notice we're flushed, which creates more self-consciousness. There's no way to prevent this response through willpower because it's happening below conscious control, but we can reduce how much it bothers us by expecting it in advance and deciding we're going to continue regardless. When we feel the heat starting, we can take a slow breath and continue with whatever we're saying rather than stopping to comment on it or apologize for it, treating it as irrelevant background noise rather than a crisis.

Some people experience a tight feeling in their chest during negotiation that makes breathing feel harder, which is the diaphragm and intercostal muscles tightening as part of the stress response. Shallow, rapid breathing both results from anxiety and makes anxiety worse by signaling to our body that we're still in danger. The intervention is deliberate breathing that's slow and goes deep into our abdomen rather than staying in our upper chest. Before starting a negotiation, we can take three breaths where we count to four on the inhale, hold for four, count to four on the exhale, and hold for four, which activates the parasympathetic nervous system and slightly reduces the baseline anxiety we're starting from.

The urge to backtrack immediately after we've said a number or made a request is almost universal among conflict-averse negotiators, and it sounds like "but if that doesn't work I could do less" or "I'm open to other options" or "what do you think?" The phrase "what do you think" is particularly dangerous after we've stated our terms because it invites them to tell us no without having to volunteer it, essentially doing their negotiating work for them. If we've prepared a script and practiced staying silent after our request, we need to be aware that the backtrack reflex will show up and we need to actively resist it by biting our tongue if necessary.

When they respond to our request with questions rather than acceptance or rejection, our first instinct is often to interpret questions as criticism or skepticism, which triggers defensive reactions. Someone asking "how did you arrive at that number?" isn't necessarily challenging us, they might genuinely want to understand our reasoning so they can justify it to their manager or HR. Our response should give them the information they need without getting defensive: "I researched market rates on Glassdoor and Payscale for this role in this location, and the range I found was $X to $Y, so I'm asking for something in the upper part of that range based on my experience with [specific relevant skill]."

The key is answering their question directly and factually rather than interpreting it as an attack and responding with justifications about why we deserve to be paid or explanations about our financial needs. They don't care about our financial needs, they care about whether we're asking for something reasonable relative to market rates and whether we can perform at the level we're claiming. Keeping the conversation focused on market data and professional qualifications rather than personal circumstances makes it easier for them to say yes.

When they tell us they need time to think about our request or that they need to talk to their manager, our anxiety will tell us this is bad news and we should lower our ask immediately to save the situation. Actually this is neutral to positive news because they're not saying no, they're saying they need to go through a process, and that process often results in them coming back with something closer to what we asked for. Our job when they say this is to simply agree and establish a timeline: "That makes sense, I understand you need to check with others. What's the timeline for getting back to me?"

The timeline question is important because it prevents the negotiation from disappearing into an indefinite "we'll get back to you" that never happens. If they say they'll get back to us in a week, we know when to follow up if we don't hear from them. If they say they need three days, we can mark that on our calendar and prepare for the next conversation. The specificity keeps the negotiation moving forward rather than stalling out.

Crying during negotiation is the response most people fear because it feels like losing control in a way that other physical symptoms don't, and for women especially it triggers anxiety about confirming stereotypes about being too emotional for professional settings. Crying happens when our emotional regulation is overwhelmed by stress, frustration, anger, or feeling cornered, and it's not something we can prevent through willpower once it starts because the crying reflex is below conscious control just like heart rate and blushing are.

If crying starts during a negotiation, the worst thing we can do is apologize repeatedly and shut down the conversation entirely, which is what most of us want to do because we're embarrassed. The better response is brief acknowledgment that keeps the focus on the content rather than the crying: "I get emotional in high-stakes conversations, I'm fine, let's keep going." Then we continue with whatever we were saying or respond to what they were saying before we started crying. This requires enormous effort when we're already upset and now embarrassed, but it's effective because it refuses to make the crying the main event and instead treats it as a minor side effect that doesn't change the validity of what we're discussing.

Most people who witness someone crying during a professional conversation are themselves uncomfortable and looking for cues about how to respond. If we signal that we're moving past it, they'll usually follow that lead. If we make it a big deal by stopping the conversation and apologizing extensively, they'll feel they need to comfort us or end the meeting, both of which derail the negotiation. The goal is to reduce the importance of the crying as quickly as possible by treating it as unremarkable.

The physical sensation of nausea that some people experience during stressful negotiations is connected to the vagus nerve and to the gut-brain connection, where anxiety literally creates stomach discomfort. There's not much we can do about this in the moment except recognize it as a stress symptom rather than a sign that we're getting sick or that something is medically wrong. If the nausea is severe enough that we genuinely can't continue, we can ask to reschedule: "I'm not feeling well, could we continue this conversation tomorrow?" This is better than pushing through a conversation we can't focus on because of physical distress.

Shaky hands are visible when we're holding papers or trying to write notes during a negotiation, which creates self-consciousness about whether the other person notices. The solution is to keep our hands on the table or in our lap rather than holding things, and to have our notes on a laptop or tablet instead of on paper if possible because screens don't shake visibly the way paper does. If we need to sign something during the negotiation and our hands are shaking, we can wait until we're slightly calmer or we can just sign despite the shake, which honestly no one cares about as much as we think they do.

The technique of asking for a break when we're overwhelmed is underused because we feel like asking for breaks makes us look weak or uncommitted, but actually taking a break to use the bathroom or get water or just step away for five minutes is completely normal and often helps reset our nervous system enough that we can continue more effectively. The script is simple: "Could we take a five-minute break? I need to use the bathroom and grab some water." No one will say no to this request, and the break gives us time to breathe, review our notes, calm down slightly, and come back to the conversation with marginally more composure.

During the break, we can do a few things that help with nervous system regulation: splash cold water on our face or wrists, which activates the diving reflex and slightly lowers heart rate; do a few big shoulder rolls and neck stretches to release muscle tension; take those slow four-count breaths we practiced; and review our script to remind ourselves of what we're asking for and why. The break doesn't need to be long to be helpful, even three minutes away from the conversation can make a meaningful difference in our ability to continue.

When we're negotiating over email instead of in person or on the phone, we lose the physical symptoms that make in-person negotiation so challenging, but we gain the anxiety of waiting for their response and the tendency to overthink and revise our emails excessively before sending them. Email negotiation can actually be easier for extremely anxious people because it removes the real-time performance pressure, but it comes with the temptation to be overly apologetic or to hedge our requests more than we would in a script we practiced out loud.

The rule for email negotiation is to write our message, save it as a draft, wait at least an hour, come back and read it one more time looking specifically for apologetic language or excessive hedging, remove any instances of "sorry" or "if that's okay" or "I hope this doesn't seem," and then send it without further revision. The waiting period prevents us from sending emails when we're at peak anxiety, when we're most likely to undermine ourselves with our language choices.

The physical symptoms we experience during negotiation are not signs that we're not cut out for this or that we should give up on getting fair compensation. They're signs that our body is doing what bodies do under social stress, which is activate all the systems designed to protect us from danger even though salary negotiation isn't actually dangerous. Managing these symptoms isn't about eliminating them, it's about continuing to execute our plan despite them, which gets marginally easier with practice but never becomes comfortable.

The first negotiation will be the hardest because everything is new and we have no evidence that we can survive it. The second negotiation will still be hard but we'll have the first one as proof that the worst case scenarios we imagine don't actually happen. The third and fourth get progressively less paralyzing not because the physical symptoms go away but because we build tolerance for discomfort and confidence that we can function despite it. This is why starting with lower-stakes practice negotiations makes sense, because we build the skill of working through physical panic in situations where the financial consequences are smaller.

# When They Say No and What Comes Next

The first no in a negotiation is almost never the actual end of the conversation, but most of us treat it as final because we're so relieved to have a resolution, any resolution, that we accept it immediately and move on. When a hiring manager says "that's outside our range" or our boss says "we can't do raises right now," our instinct is to say "okay, I understand" and drop the subject entirely, which means we've negotiated ourselves down to their first position without exploring whether that position is actually fixed or whether there's room to discuss other options.

What no usually means is no to that specific thing we just asked for, not no to the entire conversation about compensation. If we asked for $85,000 and they said no, that doesn't mean they can't do $82,000 or that they can't add a signing bonus or that they can't improve the PTO package. It means they're pushing back on our specific request to see if we're serious or if we'll immediately fold, which is a standard negotiation move that's designed to test resolve. The people who accept the first no and give up are leaving money on the table that was available if they'd just continued the conversation.

The response to a salary no is to ask what number would work rather than accepting that no number will work: "I understand that's outside your typical range. What would work for this role given my background?" This question forces them to put a number on the table rather than just rejecting ours, which gives us information about how far apart we actually are. If they say $78,000 and we asked for $85,000, we know we're $7,000 apart and we can decide whether to meet in the middle or explore other compensation components. If they say they can't go above $72,000 and we asked for $85,000, we're far enough apart that we might need to walk away or we might need to get creative about other benefits that close the gap.

When they say the salary is truly fixed with no flexibility at all, which happens in government roles, union positions, or companies with extremely rigid pay bands, our response is to shift immediately to other components: "I understand the base salary is set at $72,000 and there's no flexibility there. Let's talk about the rest of the package. I'm interested in discussing signing bonus, PTO, professional development budget, stock options if available, and remote work flexibility. Where might we find some room?"

This framing acknowledges their constraint on base salary without accepting that the entire compensation package is therefore non-negotiable. Even in the most rigid systems, there's usually flexibility somewhere, and our job is to find where that flexibility lives. The salary might be locked but maybe they can do an extra week of vacation, which has real value even though it's not cash in our paycheck. Maybe they can't adjust the standard PTO policy but they can offer a signing bonus that's equivalent to a week's pay. Maybe they can't do any cash adjustments but they can commit to an earlier performance review than the standard cycle.

The conversation about signing bonuses specifically is worth having in detail because signing bonuses are often easier for employers to approve than salary increases, since they don't affect the ongoing budget the way permanent salary changes do. A signing bonus is one-time money that comes from a different budget line and doesn't compound into future raises and bonuses the way base salary does. If we're $5,000 apart on salary and they genuinely can't move, we can ask for a $5,000 signing bonus, which gives us that money in the first year even though it doesn't have the long-term compounding effect we'd get from higher base.

The script for signing bonus negotiation after salary is declined: "I appreciate you being transparent about the salary constraints. Would a signing bonus be possible to help close the gap? I was thinking something around $5,000 to offset the difference between what I was hoping for and what's available." The specific number we ask for should roughly correspond to the gap we were trying to close, not some arbitrary amount, because we're framing it as a solution to the problem they just created by saying no to our salary request.

PTO negotiation is particularly valuable because additional vacation days have measurable financial value plus quality of life value that's hard to quantify. Each additional day of PTO is worth our daily rate, so if we're making $80,000 per year and working 260 days accounting for weekends, each vacation day is worth about $308. An extra week is worth roughly $1,540 per year, two extra weeks is worth $3,080, and these numbers compound over time because we get that extra time off every year we're employed. The script: "On the PTO policy, I know you start at [their standard], would there be flexibility to start at [one or two weeks higher] given my experience level?"

Some companies have rigid PTO policies where everyone at a given level gets the same amount regardless of negotiation, but many companies have more flexibility than they initially suggest, particularly for senior hires or people with significant experience. The worst they can say is no, and if they say yes, we've just added meaningful value to the package that will benefit us every year going forward.

Professional development budgets are often completely overlooked in negotiation because people don't think to ask about them, but they're valuable for keeping skills current and they signal that the company invests in employee growth. A professional development budget might be $2,000 to $5,000 per year for conferences, courses, certifications, books, or professional association memberships. The script: "Does the role include a professional development budget? I'm interested in staying current with [specific relevant area], and having budget for courses and conferences would be really valuable for both my growth and my ability to contribute."

The framing here emphasizes that professional development benefits the employer by keeping us skilled and current, not just us by making us more marketable elsewhere. This is actually true, professional development makes us better at our jobs, but framing it as mutual benefit makes it easier for them to say yes than if we present it as something that only benefits us.

Stock options or equity grants are standard at startups and tech companies but are possible at other companies if we ask, and they represent real value even though they're risky and take years to vest. For someone at a startup, equity can eventually be worth more than total salary over the employment period, or it can be worth nothing if the company fails, and we need to understand that variance when evaluating it. The script: "I'm optimistic about the company's growth trajectory. What does equity look like for this role? I'd be interested in discussing an options grant as part of the package."

If they offer equity but we don't understand how it works, we need to ask specific questions before accepting the offer: What's the vesting schedule? What percentage of the company do the options represent? What's the current valuation and strike price? What happens to options if we leave before fully vested? What's the preference stack in the cap table if the company gets acquired? These questions sound technical but they're necessary to understand whether the equity is likely to have real value or whether it's essentially play money the company is using to reduce cash compensation.

Remote work flexibility has become a major negotiation point and can be worth substantial money in terms of commute costs, time savings, and flexibility for personal responsibilities. If the role is advertised as in-office and we want hybrid or remote, we need to make a case for why remote work makes sense for this specific role rather than just stating our preference. The script: "I'm most productive when I have focused time for [type of work this role involves], and I find I can do that best with [number] days per week working remotely. Given that much of the work is [async collaboration, independent project work, whatever is true], would hybrid work with [specific schedule] be possible?"

The key is connecting our remote work request to outcomes that matter to them, not just to what we prefer. If we can demonstrate that remote work makes us more productive or that the role doesn't require constant in-person presence, they're more likely to agree than if we just say we don't want to commute.

Title negotiation is often overlooked because people assume titles are as fixed as the organizational chart, but titles actually have more flexibility than most other components and they have real value for future marketability even when they don't change our current paycheck. If we're being offered Associate and we have the experience for Senior Associate, negotiating the title bump costs the company nothing immediately but makes us more attractive to future employers and potentially affects our trajectory within the current company. The script: "Given the scope of responsibilities and my experience level, would it make sense to structure this as a [next level title] role rather than [level they offered]? I'm thinking both about internal positioning and about how the role translates externally."

When they've said no to salary and we've explored all the other components and they're still not willing to move on anything, we're in a genuine take-it-or-leave-it situation. At this point we need to evaluate the offer against our minimum acceptable terms that we determined before starting negotiation, and we need to decide whether to accept, walk away, or ask for time to think. The script for asking for time: "I appreciate you working with me on this. Let me take 24 hours to review everything and make sure I'm thinking clearly about the decision. I'll get back to you tomorrow by [specific time]."

Almost every employer will agree to a 24-hour delay, and if they won't, that's information about what it would be like to work for them. The time gives us space to evaluate the offer when we're not in the middle of the stressful conversation, to talk it through with people we trust if that's helpful, and to check back in with our minimum acceptable terms to see if the final offer meets them.

If the final offer is above our minimum and we decide to accept it even though it's not what we initially hoped for, we accept cleanly without relitigating the terms or expressing disappointment: "I'm excited to accept the offer and join the team. Looking forward to starting on [date]." If the final offer is below our minimum, we need to be prepared to walk away, which is terrifying for conflict-averse people but necessary if we're going to have boundaries that mean anything. The script for declining: "I appreciate the time you've spent discussing this with me. Unfortunately the compensation doesn't work for me at this point. I hope we can stay in touch for future opportunities."

This response is professional and leaves the door open without being apologetic or over-explaining our decision. We don't owe them a detailed explanation of why their offer doesn't work, and providing one often leads to them trying to address our concerns in ways that might muddy our decision. Clean decline, brief and polite, is the move.

Walking away from an offer after negotiating is actually less common than anxious people fear because most negotiations do result in some movement from both sides, but it needs to be an option we're genuinely willing to exercise or we have no leverage at all. If they know or sense that we'll accept whatever they offer because we're too afraid to walk away, they have no incentive to improve the terms. Our willingness to leave if the terms don't work is what makes negotiation possible.

The situation where we're negotiating a raise with a current employer and they say no is particularly difficult because we can't just walk away without losing our job, and threatening to leave without a real outside offer is risky. When a manager says no to our raise request, our response is to ask for specificity about why and what would need to change: "I appreciate you being honest about that. Can you help me understand what would need to be different for this to be possible? Is it about timing, metrics I need to hit, budget constraints, or something else?"

This question forces them to articulate their reasoning, which gives us information about whether this is something we can influence or whether it's entirely out of our control. If they say we need to wait until the next budget cycle, we know timing is the issue and we can ask what we should be documenting and accomplishing in the meantime to justify the raise when budget opens up. If they say budget is frozen company-wide, we know it's not about our performance and we can ask about non-financial adjustments like title or expanded responsibilities. If they say our performance needs to improve, we need specific examples of what improvement looks like so we have clear targets.

The response when they cite performance concerns is: "I want to make sure I understand what success looks like. What specific improvements or accomplishments would support a salary increase to [our target] at the next review? I'd like to be clear on the expectations so I can focus on meeting them." This pins them down to concrete metrics rather than vague "we need to see more" language that gives us nothing actionable.

If our manager can't or won't articulate what would need to change for them to approve a raise, that's actually valuable information because it suggests the no isn't about anything we can control through better performance. At that point we're making a decision about whether to stay at current compensation or start looking for external opportunities, and both options are legitimate depending on our circumstances and risk tolerance.

The conversation after we've accepted an offer, whether it was the result of successful negotiation or accepting terms that weren't what we hoped for, should include questions about the next raise cycle and the path to advancement. We've just had a negotiation conversation so continuing in that frame while it's still open is easier than trying to restart it months later. The script: "Now that we've settled on terms, I wanted to ask about the review and raise cycle. When does the first review happen, and what metrics matter most for compensation increases going forward?"

This question sets expectations that we'll be continuing to think about compensation growth, not just accepting this starting point as permanent, and it gives us information about how the company handles raises. If they say raises happen annually based on performance reviews, we know we need to document accomplishments throughout the year to support our case at review time. If they say raises are at manager discretion with no formal cycle, we know we'll need to initiate these conversations ourselves rather than waiting for a structured process.

The reality that most people don't want to hear is that one successful negotiation doesn't solve the compensation gap permanently. We negotiate our starting salary and get it to a better place, and then we need to negotiate raises, and then we need to negotiate the next job offer, and the pattern continues throughout our career. Treating negotiation as something we do once and then never again means we'll fall behind market rates within a few years because most standard raises don't keep pace with what we could get by changing jobs and negotiating new offers.

This doesn't mean we need to job hop constantly, it means we need to treat compensation as something that requires active management rather than something that happens to us based on employer generosity. Whether we're negotiating internally for raises or externally for new positions, the skill set is the same: research market rates, document our value, prepare scripts, manage our physical panic, and persist through initial no responses until we either get to acceptable terms or confirm that terms we can accept aren't available.

## The Gender Problem We Can't Negotiate Our Way Out Of

Women now negotiate job offers at higher rates than men, 54% versus 44% in recent studies of MBA graduates between 2015 and 2019, which completely destroys the myth that women don't ask or that the pay gap exists because women are too timid to negotiate. Women are asking, and they're asking more than men are, but they still earn less because when they ask they get told no more often and because the initial offers they receive before any negotiation are lower. The problem isn't individual behavior at this point, it's systemic bias in how identical negotiation behavior gets interpreted and responded to based on gender.

The backlash effect is real and measurable and it shows up in hiring decisions and performance evaluations and promotion opportunities. When women negotiate assertively using the same language and tactics that men use with no penalty, women get rated as less likable, less desirable as colleagues, and less likely to be team players. These ratings aren't just perception with no consequences, they translate into actual decisions about who gets hired and who gets advancement opportunities. Women who negotiate successfully might get higher starting salaries but they also might get marked as difficult in ways that affect their trajectory over the next several years.

The specific research that demonstrates this comes from studies where identical scripts were presented to evaluators with only the gender of the negotiator changed. When "John" asked for higher salary using specific language, evaluators found him appropriately assertive and confident. When "Jennifer" asked for the same salary using the exact same words, evaluators found her demanding and not a team player. The identical behavior produced opposite evaluations based solely on the gender of the person doing it, which means the standard advice to negotiate assertively and know our worth fundamentally misunderstands the problem women face.

This backlash creates an impossible bind where not negotiating means falling behind financially but negotiating means potential social and career costs that accumulate over time. A woman who negotiates aggressively for her starting salary might get the higher number but then find herself excluded from key projects or passed over for promotions because she's been categorized as difficult. A woman who doesn't negotiate avoids the immediate social penalty but ends up on a lower salary trajectory that compounds into significant lifetime earnings loss. Neither option is good, which is why framing this as an individual choice problem rather than a systemic bias problem is misleading.

The field experiment in Thailand that gave negotiation training to women and then tracked outcomes found that women who received training negotiated more often but actually ended up with lower salaries on average than women who didn't receive the training. The researchers concluded that negotiation training for women can backfire when the underlying bias in how negotiation is received remains unchanged. Teaching women to negotiate like men doesn't help if the system punishes women for behaving like men, which is apparently what happens when women follow standard negotiation advice without accounting for gender dynamics.

The communal framing strategy that sometimes works for women is presenting negotiation as collaborative problem-solving rather than adversarial demand-making. Instead of "I want $85,000," framing it as "based on my research and what I'm bringing to the team, $85,000 seems like the right number for this role, does that work?" The difference is subtle but meaningful: the first version centers our individual wants, the second version centers market rates and team value. Women who use communal language get hit with less backlash than women who use more direct language, though they also sometimes get lower salary increases than men using direct language.

This is frustrating because it means women have to perform additional emotional labor just to ask for fair compensation, carefully calibrating our language to avoid triggering stereotypes about demanding women, while men can be straightforward without that extra cognitive load. The fact that communal framing sometimes mitigates backlash doesn't make it fair or right that women need to use it, it's just pragmatic adaptation to bias that shouldn't exist.

The other strategy that reduces backlash for women is negotiating on behalf of others rather than for themselves. Women negotiating salary for a team member or for their department don't face the same likability penalties that they face when negotiating their own compensation. This suggests the issue isn't that people think women are bad negotiators, it's that people react negatively when women advocate for their own interests in ways that violate gender expectations about women being nurturing and selfless. When women's negotiation aligns with caretaking roles by advocating for others, the backlash disappears.

Knowing this pattern exists doesn't solve it but it does suggest some tactical approaches. When we're negotiating our own salary, we can frame some of our value in terms of what we enable for others: "My work on this project freed up 160 hours for the team to focus on higher-priority work" rather than just "I completed this project efficiently." We're not lying or downplaying our accomplishments, we're presenting them in a frame that emphasizes collaborative value rather than just individual achievement. This shouldn't be necessary, but if it reduces the penalty we face for negotiating, it's worth doing while we work on larger systemic change.

The transparency interventions that actually do reduce gender pay gaps are organizational-level changes rather than individual negotiation tactics. When companies post salary ranges in job descriptions and make it explicit that negotiation is expected and welcomed, women negotiate at nearly the same rates as men and the gender gap in outcomes decreases significantly. When salary decisions are audited for bias and managers know their compensation decisions will be reviewed for patterns, the gap narrows. When objective criteria for raises and promotions are established and enforced, women advance at rates closer to men.

These interventions work because they change the system rather than asking women to individually negotiate better in a system that's biased against them. The problem was never that women don't ask, the problem is that when women ask they face barriers and penalties that men don't face. Fixing this requires changing how organizations make compensation decisions, not teaching more negotiation workshops for women.

The current date is 2026, and some companies have started removing negotiation from their hiring process entirely by posting final offers that aren't open to discussion. This sounds like it would hurt strong negotiators who could get more by asking, but the data suggests it actually reduces pay gaps because it removes the opportunity for bias to affect who gets higher offers based on who negotiates and how those negotiations are received. When everyone gets the same offer for the same role and experience level, initial pay gaps based on gender or race largely disappear.

Not all companies are willing to do this because it requires salary transparency and standardization that many organizations resist, but the companies that have implemented it report that it simplifies hiring and reduces complaints about fairness. For job seekers, seeing posted final offers that aren't negotiable is actually helpful information because it eliminates the anxiety about whether to negotiate and the risk of backlash for trying.

The broader conversation about gender and negotiation has to include the fact that salary discussions are only one moment in a career trajectory that's affected by gender bias at every stage. Women get hired at lower rates than men for senior positions even when their qualifications are identical. Women get promoted more slowly than men even when their performance ratings are the same. Women get assigned to lower-visibility projects that don't lead to advancement. Women take career breaks for caregiving more often than men and face penalties when returning to work that men who take similar breaks don't face.

Negotiation can improve women's individual outcomes marginally but it can't fix structural problems that compound over decades. The salary gap for MBA graduates starts at 88% of male earnings and drops to 63% ten years later, and that widening isn't primarily because women stop negotiating at year five, it's because women hit barriers to advancement that men don't hit or they take parenting-related career pauses that affect trajectory in ways that men's similar pauses don't.

The emphasis on negotiation as the solution to the gender pay gap can actually be harmful because it places responsibility on individual women to fix a problem they didn't create and can't solve alone. When we tell women they earn less because they don't negotiate enough, we're implying they're partially at fault for their own pay gap, which is both inaccurate and demoralizing. Women negotiate plenty. The system responds to women's negotiation differently than it responds to men's negotiation, and that's the problem.

This doesn't mean women shouldn't negotiate, it means we need to be clear-eyed about what negotiation can and can't accomplish. Negotiating can get us higher starting salaries and larger raises than we'd get by passively accepting what's offered. Negotiating can close some of the gap between what we make and what men in similar roles make. Negotiating gives us practice advocating for ourselves in professional contexts, which is valuable regardless of the financial outcome. But negotiating won't close the systemic pay gap, and pretending it will sets women up for frustration and self-blame when they negotiate well and still end up behind male peers.

The question of whether to negotiate knowing that backlash is a real risk is one each woman has to answer based on her own circumstances and risk tolerance. Some of us decide the financial benefit of negotiating is worth the potential social cost, and we negotiate anyway while being strategic about how we frame requests. Some of us decide the social and career costs are too high in our particular workplace or industry, and we focus energy on other advancement strategies like changing jobs more frequently. Both choices are legitimate responses to a system that penalizes us for behavior it rewards in men.

What we shouldn't do is blame ourselves or other women for making either choice. The woman who negotiates aggressively and faces backlash didn't do it wrong, she's dealing with bias. The woman who doesn't negotiate because she's calculated that the cost outweighs the benefit in her situation isn't leaving money on the table through timidity, she's making a strategic decision based on real constraints. The enemy isn't our individual negotiation choices or lack thereof, it's the system that forces us to make these calculations in the first place.

The advice in earlier chapters about scripts and preparation and managing panic applies to women who decide to negotiate, and it's valuable precisely because preparation and clear scripts can reduce some of the improvisational risk that might trigger bias. When we're reading from a carefully worded script that uses communal framing and market data, we're less likely to accidentally say something that gets interpreted as demanding or aggressive than when we're improvising under stress. The scripts aren't going to eliminate backlash entirely but they might reduce the likelihood of triggering the worst reactions.

Women who are in positions to hire and manage others have a specific responsibility to be aware of these dynamics and to actively counteract them in our own decision-making. When we're evaluating negotiation from job candidates, we need to check whether we're responding differently to men and women who make similar requests. When we're making compensation decisions for our teams, we need to audit whether we're consistently offering women lower starting salaries than men with similar backgrounds. When we're advocating for promotions and raises, we need to notice whether we're holding women to higher standards of performance than men at the same level.

This isn't about giving women special treatment or lowering standards, it's about recognizing that our default judgments are affected by bias and actively correcting for that bias in how we make decisions. Most of us aren't consciously sexist, but we've all absorbed cultural messages about gender that affect how we interpret identical behavior from men and women, and those messages operate automatically unless we deliberately interrupt them.

The long-term solution to gendered negotiation dynamics is cultural change that makes assertiveness in women as acceptable as assertiveness in men, organizational practices that reduce opportunities for bias to affect compensation decisions, and legal frameworks that hold companies accountable for pay gaps that can't be explained by legitimate job-related factors. None of these changes happen quickly and none of them absolve us of navigating the current system while working toward a better one.

Women reading this who are preparing to negotiate should do so with open eyes about the possible costs and with strategic thinking about how to minimize backlash through framing and timing. We should also be doing it with the knowledge that we're not alone in facing these dynamics, that the difficulty isn't a personal failing, and that negotiating despite the challenges is one way of pushing back against systems that want us to accept less than we're worth. The act of negotiating, even when it's hard and even when we face backlash, is a small form of resistance against norms that benefit from our silence.

The intersectionality of gender with race, class, and other identities compounds these dynamics in ways that are important to acknowledge even though they're difficult to address through individual negotiation tactics. Women of color face both gender bias and racial bias in compensation decisions, and the research shows that Black women and Latina women face larger pay gaps than white women do. Asian American women's pay gap varies significantly by ethnicity and immigration status, with some groups earning close to parity with white men while others face substantial gaps.

The specific stereotypes that affect different groups of women shape how negotiation behavior gets interpreted. Black women who negotiate assertively may get coded as aggressive or angry in ways that trigger racist stereotypes about Black women being difficult or threatening. Asian women who negotiate may face stereotypes about being submissive or not suited for leadership, which means their negotiation gets dismissed as out of character rather than taken seriously. Latina women face stereotypes about being emotional or family-focused rather than career-driven, which can affect how seriously their compensation requests are taken.

These layered biases mean that negotiation advice needs to account for more than just gender, and the communal framing strategies that might help white women reduce backlash might not be sufficient or appropriate for women dealing with racial bias on top of gender bias. There's no simple script that works universally because the bias we're navigating varies based on who we are and who's evaluating us.

Disability status adds another layer where women with disabilities face both gender pay gaps and disability pay gaps, and negotiation becomes complicated by concerns about whether asking for accommodations or flexibility will be seen as demanding special treatment. The same negotiation that a non-disabled person can frame as professional assertiveness might be interpreted as a disabled person being difficult or needing too much support. The fear of triggering these stereotypes can make negotiation feel even more risky for disabled women than for non-disabled women.

LGBTQ women face their own specific barriers where sexual orientation or gender identity might affect whether they're read as appropriately feminine or whether their negotiation gets interpreted through stereotypes about queer women being too aggressive or not fitting traditional professional norms. Trans women navigating negotiation have to deal with potential transphobia on top of the regular gender bias, and the calculation about whether negotiation is worth the risk includes concerns about whether it will draw negative attention to their gender identity.

The point of naming these intersecting identities isn't to create a hierarchy of who has it worst or to suggest that some women shouldn't bother negotiating. The point is that negotiation advice needs to acknowledge that not all women face identical circumstances, and the strategies that work for women with relative privilege might not be sufficient or appropriate for women facing multiple forms of bias simultaneously.

What this means practically is that women from marginalized groups need to make even more calculated decisions about when and how to negotiate, and they need support systems that recognize the additional barriers they're navigating. It's not enough to tell Black women or disabled women or trans women to negotiate like white cis non-disabled women do, because the reception will be different and the costs might be higher.

The mentorship gap affects women's access to negotiation advice and advocacy in ways that compound over careers. Women, especially women of color, are less likely to have senior mentors who can give them inside information about compensation ranges, advocate for them in promotion discussions, or coach them through negotiation conversations. Men are more likely to have access to informal networks where compensation information gets shared and where senior people invest in developing their careers. This information asymmetry means women often go into negotiations with less knowledge about what's actually possible and less organizational support for their requests.

Building networks and finding mentors who will share this information openly is valuable but it's also work that takes time and energy that could be going toward actual job performance, and it's work that men often don't have to do because the networks and mentorship happen more automatically for them. The unfairness of having to build support systems that should already exist is real, but the practical reality is that we're more likely to negotiate successfully when we have people inside organizations who can tell us what the actual ranges are and who will advocate for us in rooms we're not in.

The pregnancy and motherhood penalty is well-documented and affects negotiation in specific ways. Women who are visibly pregnant or who have young children face assumptions about their commitment and availability that men with children don't face, and these assumptions affect both initial salary offers and responses to negotiation attempts. A pregnant woman negotiating for higher salary might face skepticism about whether she'll actually stay long-term or whether she'll be able to maintain her performance after having children. A mother negotiating for a raise might hear that she should be grateful to have flexibility rather than asking for more money.

These assumptions are often unstated but they shape compensation decisions in ways that are hard to identify and challenge. A hiring manager might not consciously think "she's pregnant so I'll offer her less," but they might have unconscious concerns about return on investment or future availability that lead them to make a lower offer or to push back harder on her negotiation than they would with a non-pregnant candidate. The effect is the same even if the bias isn't explicit or intentional.

The career interruptions that women are more likely to take for caregiving reasons affect negotiation in the resume gap sense where we're trying to explain time away from paid work, and in the psychological sense where we might feel less confident about our market value after time away. The advice to anchor salary requests on current market rates rather than on what we made before a career break is especially important for women returning from parenting or caregiving breaks, because our previous salary is often years out of date and doesn't reflect what we're worth now.

The confidence gap that gets discussed in career advice often misdiagnoses the problem. Women don't negotiate less because they're less confident, they negotiate less in some contexts because they've accurately assessed that negotiation carries higher risks for them than it does for men. What gets called lack of confidence is often actually appropriate risk assessment. When negotiating successfully requires not just asking but asking in a way that doesn't trigger gender stereotypes, and when the cost of triggering those stereotypes includes real career consequences, it's rational to hesitate.

The solution isn't confidence training or telling women to "lean in" more aggressively. The solution is changing organizational practices so that negotiation doesn't carry gendered costs, and in the meantime, giving women accurate information about the risks they're navigating and the strategies that might help mitigate those risks without requiring them to become someone they're not.

The exhaustion of having to negotiate more carefully than men do, of having to manage perceptions and frame requests perfectly and worry about backlash in addition to actually making the case for fair compensation, is real and it's part of the cost that doesn't show up in pay gap statistics. Even when women succeed in negotiating higher salaries, the emotional and cognitive labor required to do it is greater than what men have to expend for similar outcomes. This cumulative exhaustion over a career is part of why women leave certain industries or opt out of advancement opportunities even when they're technically available.

Acknowledging this exhaustion and these barriers doesn't mean giving up on negotiation. It means being realistic about what we're asking women to do when we tell them to negotiate their way to equal pay, and being honest that negotiation is one tool among many but not a complete solution to systemic inequality. Women should negotiate when the calculation makes sense for their situation, and they should do it with support and resources and realistic expectations about what's achievable through individual action within biased systems.

## Starting Small When the Stakes Are Lower

We don't build negotiation tolerance by jumping straight into salary conversations that could cost us hundreds of thousands of dollars if we mess them up. We build it by practicing on situations where rejection won't destroy us financially and where the emotional stakes are lower even though the discomfort is similar. The goal isn't to become comfortable with negotiation, which probably won't happen regardless of how much we practice, but to build evidence that we can survive asking for things and that the worst case scenarios we imagine rarely materialize.

The practice negotiations that work best are ones where we're asking strangers or near-strangers for something, because the relationship risk is minimal. If a hotel desk clerk says no to our request for late checkout, we're not going to see that person again and the rejection has no ongoing consequences. If a car dealer won't come down on price, we can walk away and try a different dealer without any lasting impact. These low-relationship-stakes scenarios let us experience the physical discomfort of asking without the additional fear of damaging important professional relationships.

Car buying is one of the most accessible practice grounds because everyone expects negotiation and dealers have built-in flexibility in their pricing. Walking onto a car lot knowing we're going to negotiate the price creates the same anxiety symptoms we'll feel in salary negotiations: racing heart, tight chest, urge to just accept their number and escape. The difference is that if we accept a bad price on a car, it's a few thousand dollars gone but not a trajectory-altering mistake the way accepting a low salary is. The financial stakes are real enough to matter but not so high that failure is catastrophic.

The script for car negotiation is straightforward: we research what the car typically sells for using sites like TrueCar or Edmunds, we get quotes from multiple dealers, and then we tell each dealer what the lowest quote we have is and ask if they can beat it. "I've gotten quotes from three other dealers and the best one so far is $28,500 for this exact car. Can you do better than that?" This script requires us to state a number, wait for response, and potentially hear no, which is exactly the pattern we need to practice for salary negotiation.

Most car dealers will either match the competing quote or come close to it, which gives us the experience of negotiation working. Some will say they can't match it, which gives us the experience of hearing no without collapsing. Either outcome builds our tolerance for the negotiation process because we're learning that asking doesn't destroy the interaction and that hearing no doesn't mean we've committed some terrible social violation.

Furniture stores and appliance stores often have flexibility on pricing, particularly on floor models or items with minor cosmetic damage. Asking for a discount on a couch that has a small scratch requires the same skills as salary negotiation: identifying something we want, making a specific request based on justifiable reasoning, and waiting for their response without immediately backing down. The script: "I'm interested in this couch but I noticed there's a scratch on the arm. Would you be able to do 15% off the floor model price?"

The percentage we ask for should be proportional to the issue, 10-20% for minor cosmetic problems, and we should be ready to walk away if they say no, which is actually easier with furniture than with job offers because there are always other couches. The practice here is in making the ask clearly, tolerating the brief discomfort of waiting for an answer, and accepting either yes or no as just information rather than judgment about our worth.

Hotel late checkout is nearly always negotiable and costs the hotel nothing if the room isn't booked for that night, which makes it a good low-stakes practice ground. The script is simple: "I'm checking out tomorrow and my flight isn't until 3 p.m., would late checkout be possible?" Most hotels will say yes, some will charge a fee, very few will give us a flat no. The practice is in asking for something that feels like a favor when it's actually a standard request they handle constantly.

Service provider negotiations like asking for a better rate on internet or phone service require similar skills but add the element of being willing to potentially cancel if they won't improve our terms. The script: "I've been a customer for [timeframe] and I'm looking at other providers who are offering [lower price or better service]. I'd prefer to stay but I need my rate to be competitive. What can you do to keep my business?" This negotiation involves mild confrontation because we're essentially threatening to leave, but it's confrontation with a stranger at a company rather than with someone we have to maintain an ongoing relationship with.

Most retention departments for phone, internet, and cable companies have authority to offer discounts or upgrades because keeping existing customers is cheaper than acquiring new ones. When we call prepared to negotiate our rate, we're likely to get at least some concession, which gives us positive reinforcement that asking for better terms works. The few times they can't or won't negotiate, we get practice hearing no and deciding whether to follow through on leaving.

Negotiating with landlords about rent or lease terms is higher stakes than negotiating with car dealers but still lower stakes than salary because housing is easier to change than jobs and the relationship with a landlord is more transactional than the relationship with an employer. When our lease is coming up for renewal and rent is increasing, we can negotiate based on being a reliable tenant who pays on time and maintains the property. The script: "I've been a good tenant for [timeframe], always paid on time, never had complaints. The market rate for similar apartments is $X and you're proposing $Y. Could we meet somewhere in the middle at $Z?"

This negotiation might work or might not depending on the local market and the landlord's constraints, but either way we're practicing making a case based on our value and on market research, waiting for response, and potentially hearing no without it meaning we're bad at negotiating. Some landlords will reduce the increase or throw in upgrades like new appliances, some will hold firm on their number, and both outcomes give us useful experience.

Asking for discounts at small businesses where we're regular customers puts us in the position of negotiating with someone we have a relationship with, which starts to approximate the dynamic of salary negotiation with an employer. If we're at a coffee shop where we go daily, asking if they offer a discount for regulars or if they can add an extra shot for free occasionally because we're there so often, requires navigating the line between relationship and transaction. The script: "I'm in here almost every day, do you do any kind of regular customer discount or loyalty program?"

Most small businesses appreciate loyal customers and will find some way to acknowledge that loyalty, whether it's formal discounts or informal extras. The practice is in asking for something based on relationship value without coming across as entitled or demanding, which is a balance we also need in salary negotiations where we're asking for more money while maintaining that we're excited about the work and value the opportunity.

Asking for free samples or upgrades when we're making purchases gives us practice with casual negotiation that has no real downside. At a makeup counter or food store, asking "are there samples available?" or "would you be willing to throw in a small one of this other product since I'm buying the large size?" costs us nothing if they say no and occasionally gets us free things if they say yes. This isn't about getting free stuff as much as it's about building comfort with the act of asking for things we want rather than just accepting what's offered.

The cumulative effect of doing these small negotiations is that we're building a reference bank of experiences where asking for things wasn't catastrophic. We asked the hotel for late checkout and they said yes without making us feel bad about asking. We negotiated internet service and got our bill reduced by $20 a month. We asked for a discount on furniture and they gave us 10% off. Each of these small wins creates evidence that contradicts our anxiety's insistence that asking for more will result in rejection and judgment.

The nos we hear during practice negotiations are equally valuable because they show us that rejection isn't the end of the world. The car dealer said they couldn't match the competing quote and we walked away and bought from someone else. The landlord said the rent increase was firm and we decided whether that was acceptable or whether we needed to move. The coffee shop said they don't do regular customer discounts and we continued going there anyway because we liked their coffee. None of these nos destroyed us or ruined the relationship permanently.

Starting with strangers and moving gradually toward negotiations with people we have relationships with creates a progression where the difficulty increases slowly rather than jumping straight to the hardest version. Negotiating with a stranger at a car dealership is easier than negotiating with a landlord we see regularly, which is easier than negotiating with a boss we work with daily. As we build tolerance through the easier scenarios, the harder ones become slightly more manageable because we have evidence that the basic skills transfer.

The time investment in practice negotiations isn't negligible but it's also not years of work before we're ready for real salary conversations. Doing five to ten practice negotiations across a few months gives us enough varied experience that we have some confidence going into higher-stakes talks. This might mean negotiating our internet bill, asking for late checkout at two different hotels, negotiating with a car dealer even if we're not buying immediately, asking for a discount on furniture or electronics, and negotiating with our landlord about something minor like including parking or allowing a pet.

Some people find practice negotiations feel artificial because they're negotiating for the sake of practice rather than because they genuinely care about the outcome, and this artificiality makes the practice less useful. The solution is to only practice on things we actually want or that would genuinely benefit us if we got them. If we actually want late checkout because our flight is late afternoon, the practice is real. If we actually need to reduce our internet bill to save money, the negotiation is real. The practice becomes more valuable when the outcomes matter to us even though the stakes are lower than salary.

Practicing with a friend or partner who can role-play as the employer or hiring manager is useful for some people and counterproductive for others. The benefit is getting to rehearse the conversation including the back-and-forth that happens when the other person responds to our initial request. The drawback is that practice with someone we trust doesn't replicate the stress response we'll have with an actual stranger who has power over our income. We can get partway there by asking our practice partner to push back harder than we expect, to seem skeptical of our requests, to make us justify our asks, so we're experiencing some version of the challenge rather than just having them agree to everything immediately.

Recording ourselves practicing negotiation scripts and listening back is uncomfortable but educational because we hear ourselves the way others hear us. We might notice we're apologizing more than we realized, or using filler words like "um" and "like" that make us sound uncertain, or rushing through the important parts because we want to get past them quickly. These are all things we can work on adjusting before the real negotiation, which makes the real conversation marginally more likely to go well.

The goal of practice isn't perfection and it isn't becoming someone who loves negotiation. The goal is building just enough tolerance and evidence that we can execute a negotiation script when it matters without our anxiety completely shutting us down. We're not trying to become natural negotiators or people who find this energizing rather than depleting. We're trying to move from "absolutely cannot do this under any circumstances" to "can do this when necessary even though it's terrible," which is a meaningful shift that translates into real money over a career.

The progression from practice negotiations to real salary negotiations doesn't have to be immediate or dramatic. After doing several practice negotiations and surviving them, we might start with negotiating a minor raise or a small benefit at our current job before attempting to negotiate a new job offer. Or we might negotiate a consulting rate or a freelance contract before negotiating full-time employment. The incremental approach lets us build confidence and skills gradually rather than requiring us to be ready for the highest-stakes conversation right away.

Some people will do all the practice negotiations and still feel completely unprepared for real salary negotiation because the stakes are so much higher that the practice doesn't transfer cleanly. This is normal and it doesn't mean the practice was wasted. The practice gives us proof that we've asked for things before and survived, even if the emotional experience of salary negotiation feels entirely different. Having that proof somewhere in our memory is better than going into salary negotiation having never negotiated anything before and having no evidence that we're capable of doing it at all.

The practice also builds familiarity with the basic mechanics of negotiation that do transfer regardless of stakes: researching market rates or typical terms, preparing what we're going to say in advance, stating our request clearly, staying quiet after we make the request, responding to pushback without immediately caving, and accepting the outcome without excessive self-judgment regardless of whether we got what we asked for. These mechanics are the same whether we're negotiating with a car dealer or a potential employer, even though the emotional intensity is completely different.

## What to Do With the Money After We Get It

We negotiate successfully, we get the higher salary or the raise or the signing bonus, and then many of us immediately absorb the extra money into our regular spending in ways that don't match why we asked for it in the first place. The psychological trap of lifestyle inflation is that we fought hard to get an extra $8,000 per year, and then within six months we're spending exactly that much more on a nicer apartment or a better car or more frequent dining out, and we end up in the exact same financial position we were in before except now with slightly nicer stuff.

This isn't a moral failing and it's not about lacking discipline, it's about human psychology and the way increased income creates increased reference points for what feels normal. When we're making $68,000, spending $1,200 on rent feels like a lot and spending $1,500 feels extravagant. When we're making $76,000, spending $1,200 feels like we're depriving ourselves and spending $1,500 feels reasonable. Our sense of what's appropriate scales with income unless we deliberately intervene to keep it from scaling, and most people don't intervene because they're not thinking about the long-term implications at the moment they're deciding whether to upgrade their housing or their car.

The compound effects we discussed earlier about how small salary differences create massive wealth differences over decades only work if the extra money gets saved and invested rather than spent immediately. Someone who negotiates their salary from $68,000 to $73,000 and then spends the extra $5,000 every year ends up with zero additional retirement savings compared to someone making $68,000. The negotiation effort was wasted from a wealth-building perspective because the money went to consumption rather than investment. This doesn't mean consumption is bad, it means we should be conscious about the choice we're making between current consumption and future wealth.

Deciding ahead of time what the extra money from negotiation is for creates a plan that we can execute automatically rather than making spending decisions in the moment when we're tired or stressed or being advertised to. Before we negotiate, while we're still at our current salary, we decide: if I get an extra

$5,000 per year, I'm going to put $4,000 into retirement accounts and $1,000 into an emergency fund. Or: half goes to debt payoff, half goes to saving for a house down payment. Or: all of it goes to retirement because I'm behind on savings and I can maintain my current lifestyle fine. The specific allocation matters less than having the allocation decided before the money shows up.

Automatic transfers are the implementation mechanism that makes the plan stick. As soon as the first paycheck with the higher salary hits our account, we set up automatic transfers to savings and investment accounts that move the extra money out before we have a chance to spend it. If our previous monthly take-home was $4,250 and our new monthly take-home is $4,650, we set up a $400 automatic transfer to our retirement account or savings account or wherever we decided it should go. That money moves out on the same day our paycheck arrives, and we never see it in our checking account where it might get spent on random things.

The reason this works is that it removes the ongoing decision-making from the equation. We're not testing our willpower every two weeks by looking at extra money in our checking account and trying to decide not to spend it. We made the decision once, when we were thinking clearly, and then we automated it so our future stressed or tempted self doesn't have to remake the decision repeatedly. Automation is how we bridge the gap between our intentions about money and our actual behavior with money.

For people who negotiated higher base salary, the extra money shows up in every paycheck, which means the automatic transfer can be set up as a percentage or fixed amount that happens regularly. For people who negotiated a signing bonus, the money arrives as a lump sum, which creates different challenges because lump sums feel like windfall money that's somehow separate from regular income, and we tend to spend windfall money more loosely than we spend regular salary. The solution is to treat the signing bonus like any other income and immediately move it to wherever we decided it should go rather than letting it sit in checking where we'll spend it incrementally.

The question of how much of a salary increase to save versus how much to spend on improved quality of life is one each person has to answer based on their current financial situation and values, but the default shouldn't be spending all of it just because that's what happens when we don't make an explicit plan. If we're drowning in debt or have no emergency fund or are way behind on retirement savings, the case for saving most or all of the increase is strong. If we're financially stable and genuinely improving quality of life in meaningful ways by spending the increase, that's a legitimate choice. The important thing is making the choice consciously rather than drifting into spending simply because the money is there.

The retirement account contribution is particularly important because it's where compound returns do most of their work and because many employers match contributions up to a certain percentage. If we negotiated salary from $68,000 to $73,000 and we were previously contributing 3% to our 401k because that was all we could afford, we can now increase our contribution to 6% and capture the full employer match if it exists. This doubles our retirement contributions without changing our take-home much because the employer match means the account grows faster than our individual contribution alone would support.

For someone who's already maxing out employer match and contributing the full $23,000 annual limit to their 401k, the additional salary can go to other investment vehicles like a Roth IRA, a taxable brokerage account, or a Health Savings Account if they have a high-deductible health plan. The goal is to get the money invested somewhere rather than leaving it in checking where inflation slowly erodes its value and where we're tempted to spend it.

The emergency fund question matters because many people negotiating salary are doing it from a place of financial stress where they don't have savings cushion, and that stress makes the next negotiation even harder because the stakes feel impossibly high. Building three to six months of expenses in an accessible savings account creates breathing room that makes it easier to negotiate future raises or job offers because we're not negotiating from desperation. If we have six months of expenses saved, we can walk away from a bad offer. If we have nothing saved, we feel like we have to accept whatever we're offered regardless of whether it's fair.

The debt payoff calculation depends on interest rates and personal psychology. High-interest debt like credit cards at 20% annual interest should generally be prioritized over investing because the guaranteed 20% return from paying off that debt is better than the average 7-10% return from stock market investing. Student loans at 4% interest or mortgages at 3% interest are different calculations where the case for investing instead of extra debt payoff is stronger because we're likely to earn more in the market than we're paying in interest.

Some people have strong emotional responses to debt that make mathematical optimization less important than psychological relief. If having student loan debt creates constant anxiety regardless of the interest rate, using negotiated salary increases to pay off that debt faster might be worth it even if it's not the financially optimal choice. We're not robots maximizing returns, we're humans trying to build financial security in ways that don't make us miserable, and psychological factors are legitimate considerations in financial planning.

The guilt some of us feel about negotiating successfully and getting more money than others in similar roles or more money than we expected is a separate issue that shows up particularly for people who grew up without much money or who have impostor syndrome about their professional success. We negotiated, we got a higher number, and now we feel bad about it because part of us believes we don't deserve it or that getting more than others makes us greedy or that we somehow took advantage of the system. This guilt can lead to spending the extra money in self-sabotaging ways or not using it at all because using it feels like admitting we wanted it.

The antidote to guilt about successful negotiation is remembering that we negotiated to market rates, not to amounts that are unfairly high. If the market pays $75,000 for our role and experience and we negotiated to $75,000, we're getting what the work is worth, not taking advantage of anyone. The fact that some people accept $68,000 for the same work doesn't mean we should have accepted $68,000, it means those people are being underpaid and should negotiate too. Our accepting fair compensation isn't what's creating unfairness in the system, the system's tendency to underpay people who don't negotiate is what creates unfairness.

Using the extra money in ways that align with our values helps reduce the psychological discomfort around having more. If we feel guilty about earning more money, using some of it for charitable giving or helping family members or supporting causes we care about can make it feel less like pure self-interest. This isn't about earning the right to keep our salary through charitable acts, it's about recognizing that we can both earn what we're worth and use that increased earning to support things beyond ourselves.

The lifestyle inflation that happens gradually is different from the inflation that happens all at once. Gradually increasing spending as income increases over years means we might not notice we're spending more, it just feels like our life is improving in normal ways. Sudden large increases in spending right after getting a raise or new job feel more conscious but they're often driven by the impulse to celebrate or by the sense that we've earned rewards for our success. Both patterns can result in spending all the extra money instead of saving it, but the sudden version is easier to catch and adjust because it's more visible.

The specific trap of moving to a more expensive apartment or buying a more expensive car is that these are fixed monthly costs that lock in the higher spending for years. If we get an $8,000 raise and immediately move to an apartment that costs $700 more per month, we've committed $8,400 per year to housing, which is more than the entire raise. We can't easily undo this decision if we realize six months later that we'd rather be saving the money because we signed a lease or we bought a car with a loan. The reversibility of spending choices matters when thinking about lifestyle inflation.

Smaller spending increases on things like subscriptions, dining out, entertainment, and shopping are easier to adjust if we decide we want to redirect money to savings, but they're also easier to let drift because no individual increase feels significant. Adding three streaming services at $15 each per month is $540 per year, which is meaningful money that could go to an IRA, but in the moment each subscription feels like nothing. These small inflations add up faster than we think they will because we're not tracking them as a category, we're just noticing we're spending more without knowing exactly where it's going.

Tracking spending for one or two months after a salary increase can be illuminating because it shows us where the extra money is actually going rather than where we think it's going or where we intended it to go. Many people discover they're spending significantly more on discretionary purchases without having made any conscious decision to do so, just because having more money in checking creates permission to spend more freely. Seeing this pattern in data rather than just feeling vaguely like money disappears faster than it used to creates opportunity to redirect it if that's what we want to do.

The question of when to let lifestyle inflate is as important as whether to let it inflate at all. Early career is when compound returns have the longest time horizon to work, which means saving aggressively in our twenties and thirties has disproportionate impact on eventual retirement wealth compared to saving the same amounts in our forties and fifties. This suggests that keeping lifestyle relatively stable even as income increases during early career has the highest payoff, and allowing lifestyle to inflate more freely later in career when retirement accounts are already well-funded and compound returns have done most of their work makes more sense.

This doesn't mean living in poverty while young and rich so we can be comfortable when old and less able to enjoy it. It means being strategic about which lifestyle upgrades matter most to current quality of life versus which ones are just spending because we have the money. An extra $300 per month on housing might genuinely improve daily life if it means living alone instead of with roommates or living in a safer neighborhood or having space to work from home. That same $300 on a nicer car that sits in a parking lot most of the day might not improve quality of life proportionally.

The balance between current quality of life and future financial security is genuinely difficult and there's no universal right answer. Someone who grew up in poverty and is finally making decent money has different needs around allowing themselves to enjoy that money than someone who grew up comfortable and is used to financial security. Someone with chronic health issues that make the future uncertain might reasonably prioritize current quality of life over aggressive retirement saving. Someone supporting family members financially has constraints on saving that someone without those obligations doesn't have.

What we're advocating for isn't a specific savings rate or a judgment about how much is too much to spend on housing or whether anyone needs a nice car. What we're advocating for is consciousness about the choices we're making with money we fought to get through negotiation. If we decide to spend all the extra money from a raise on improved quality of life, that's legitimate as long as it's a decision we made with open eyes rather than something that happened because we didn't make any decision at all. If we decide to save all of it for retirement, that's legitimate as long as we're not depriving ourselves of reasonable current quality of life out of guilt or shame about earning more.

The intersection between negotiation and financial planning is that negotiation creates the resources that financial planning works with. We can be brilliant at budgeting and saving and investing, but if we're consistently accepting salaries $5,000 to $10,000 below market rates, we're limiting how much we have to work with regardless of how carefully we manage what we have. Conversely, we can negotiate perfectly and consistently get top-of-market salaries, but if we spend every increase immediately, we end up in the same financial position as someone who never negotiated at all.

Both skills matter, negotiation and financial management, and they work together to build the compound wealth that creates options and security over decades. Negotiation gets us the money, financial management ensures the money serves our long-term interests rather than disappearing into lifestyle inflation that doesn't meaningfully improve our lives. Getting good at one without the other is leaving the job half done.

## The Conversation We Keep Having

Negotiation isn't one conversation we have and then we're done, it's a pattern we'll repeat for the next thirty or forty years every time we change jobs or ask for a raise or take on new responsibilities. Each instance stays uncomfortable because we're asking for more money while our body is telling us that asking puts us at social risk, and that fundamental tension doesn't resolve through practice or experience. What changes with repetition is that we get slightly better at executing our plan despite the discomfort, and we accumulate evidence that the conversation itself won't kill us even though it feels like it might.

The cost of avoiding this conversation adds up silently in ways we never directly observe. We don't get a statement showing the $600,000 we didn't earn over our career because we accepted first offers without negotiating. We don't see a line item for the raises we didn't get because we waited for employers to proactively increase our pay instead of asking for what we're worth. The money just isn't there, and we compare ourselves to what we have rather than to what we could have had, so the gap feels invisible even though it's massive and real.

The numbers we've been working with throughout these chapters aren't exaggerations or best-case scenarios, they're what happens when we apply standard compound math to typical salary differences over normal career spans. A $5,000 gap at age 25 becomes $634,000 by retirement when we account for raises that build on the base and investment returns that compound over decades. Women who negotiate consistently earn $1,000,000 to $1,500,000 more than women who don't, not through dramatic one-time wins but through accumulated small percentage increases that stack year after year.

These amounts are large enough that they change retirement age, housing options, ability to help family members, capacity to weather emergencies, and general financial stress levels throughout our lives. The difference between someone who negotiated regularly and someone who didn't isn't marginal, it's the difference between financial security and ongoing financial anxiety, between retiring at 65 and working until 70, between having options and having constraints.

This isn't about becoming aggressive or confident or fundamentally different from who we are. It's about having exact words to say when our brain goes blank under stress, understanding why our body revolts against this specific conversation so we can plan around that response instead of being controlled by it, and knowing that the fifteen minutes of acute discomfort is worth hundreds of thousands of dollars over a career even though in the moment it feels like the discomfort is the only thing that's real.

The systemic problems are real and we can't negotiate our way out of them individually. Women get told no more often than men when they negotiate, initial offers to women are lower even before negotiation begins, backlash for assertiveness affects women's careers in ways it doesn't affect men's, and the pay gap widens over time through accumulated bias in promotion decisions and project assignments and whose requests get taken seriously. These are organizational and cultural problems that require organizational and cultural solutions, not better individual negotiation technique.

But we still live and work inside these systems right now, today, and while we push for structural change we also need to eat and pay rent and build retirement savings. Having scripts that work for conflict-averse people and understanding the specific challenges women face and knowing how to prepare in ways that reduce panic, these things help us navigate the current reality more effectively even though they don't fix the underlying unfairness. We can acknowledge systemic problems while still equipping ourselves to function within the system as it currently exists.

The choice in front of us is simple but not easy. We can have the conversation that makes us want to throw up, or we can leave somewhere between $400,000 and $1,000,000 on the table over the next few decades. Neither option is comfortable. One of them costs a lot more than the other. The discomfort of negotiation is acute and time-limited, it happens during specific conversations and then it's over. The cost of not negotiating is chronic and accumulating, it shows up every month in smaller paychecks and smaller retirement contributions and it compounds over the entire span of our career.

Framing it this way doesn't make negotiation less terrifying in the moment, but it does put the terror in context. Fifteen minutes of conversation where our voice shakes and our heart races and we want to escape versus decades of financial consequences from accepting whatever we're offered without asking for more. The calculation favors having the conversation even though the conversation is awful, and knowing that intellectually helps slightly when we're preparing to do it even though it doesn't eliminate the physical panic that shows up when we're actually in the negotiation.

The tools we've covered work because they acknowledge how conflict-averse people actually experience negotiation rather than pretending we can just decide to be confident and then execute perfectly. We need research that's specific enough to cite confidently. We need scripts that are complete enough to read verbatim when our brain stops working. We need preparation that moves decisions out of the high-stress moment into times when we're thinking clearly. We need permission to acknowledge our physical responses without treating them as signs we shouldn't be negotiating. We need practice on lower-stakes conversations to build evidence that asking doesn't destroy us.

None of these tools make negotiation pleasant, but they make it possible, and possible is sufficient when the alternative is accepting compensation below what we're worth for our entire career. We don't need to love negotiation or be good at it in some natural effortless way. We need to be able to execute it adequately despite finding it terrible, which is achievable through preparation and structure even for people who would genuinely rather do almost anything else.

The first negotiation will be the hardest because everything is new and unknown and we have no evidence that we can survive it. The experience will probably be as uncomfortable as we fear it will be, maybe more so, and we'll likely make mistakes or handle parts of it awkwardly. This is normal and expected and it doesn't mean we did it wrong or that we're not cut out for advocating for ourselves. It means we did something difficult that we'd never done before, and doing difficult new things is almost always messy the first time.

The second negotiation will still be hard but we'll have the first one as proof that we didn't die from the discomfort, the offer didn't get rescinded because we asked for more, the relationship didn't explode because we negotiated instead of immediately accepting their terms. Each subsequent negotiation builds on that evidence, and while they never become comfortable, they become marginally less paralyzing because we have data about outcomes rather than just catastrophic predictions.

Some negotiations will go well and we'll get close to what we asked for, and those successes will reinforce that negotiation can work in our favor financially. Some negotiations will go poorly and we'll get less than we hoped or face pushback that confirms our fears about backlash, and those experiences will be discouraging but they're also data about that specific situation rather than proof that negotiation always fails. The range of outcomes is wide, and we need enough negotiations over time to see the pattern rather than concluding from one or two instances that we know how it always works.

The relationship between negotiation and other career skills matters because negotiation isn't happening in isolation from how we perform in our jobs or how we navigate workplace relationships or how we position ourselves for opportunities. Someone who negotiates well but performs poorly won't last long regardless of their starting salary. Someone who negotiates well and performs well but doesn't build relationships or communicate effectively will hit advancement barriers that negotiation alone can't solve. Negotiation is one component of career management, important and high-impact but not sufficient by itself.

This also means that people who genuinely can't negotiate, whether due to anxiety disorders that make it impossible or workplace situations where negotiation would genuinely risk their job security or immigration status that makes job loss catastrophic, aren't doomed to poverty. They can focus on the other components of career management: performing exceptionally well, building skills that increase market value, changing jobs strategically, seeking out employers who pay fairly without requiring negotiation, and being strategic about which opportunities to pursue. These approaches won't fully compensate for never negotiating, but they can close some of the gap.

For most of us, the barrier to negotiation isn't that it's genuinely impossible but that it's uncomfortable enough that we avoid it even though we could do it if we had sufficient preparation and support. The work is in building the infrastructure that makes it possible to act despite discomfort: research, scripts, practice, understanding our physiological responses, accepting that it will always be somewhat terrible but doing it anyway because the financial consequences of not doing it are worse.

The money matters, and pretending it doesn't or treating caring about money as shallow or materialistic is a luxury that most people can't afford. Money is how we pay for housing and food and healthcare and our children's education and our parents' care and our own retirement. Money is options and security and freedom from constant financial stress. Money isn't everything but it's not nothing either, and earning what we're worth matters for our quality of life and for the lives of people who depend on us.

Negotiating for fair compensation isn't greedy or demanding or inappropriate, it's normal business practice that happens constantly in professional contexts. The fact that it feels inappropriate to us is about our particular psychology and socialization, not about the actual norms of workplace compensation discussions. Employers expect negotiation, they budget for it, they respect people who do it professionally, and they sometimes take advantage of people who don't do it by offering less than they're willing to pay and hoping it won't be questioned.

The conversation we keep having isn't going to get dramatically easier, but it does get slightly more manageable as we accumulate experience and evidence. The physical symptoms stay similar, the anxiety stays similar, but our ability to function despite them improves marginally with each negotiation we survive. This improvement is gradual enough that we might not notice it happening, but comparing how we handle our tenth negotiation to how we handled our first often reveals real growth in our capacity to execute despite discomfort.

We're not trying to become people who enjoy negotiation or who find it energizing instead of depleting. We're trying to become people who can negotiate adequately despite finding it awful, and that's achievable for most conflict-averse people if we're willing to do the preparation work and if we accept that feeling terrible during the conversation doesn't mean we're doing it wrong. The standard for success isn't feeling confident or comfortable, it's getting through the conversation and getting compensation that's closer to what we're worth than what we would have gotten by accepting the first offer without discussion.

The gap between where we are and where we could be financially is largely determined by whether we have these conversations. Everything else matters too: the work we do, the skills we build, the opportunities we pursue, the financial decisions we make with the money we earn. But the conversations where we ask for more rather than accepting what's offered are disproportionately important relative to how much time they take and how much we dread them. Fifteen minutes of conversation per negotiation, maybe ten negotiations over a career, that's two and a half hours total that determines hundreds of thousands of dollars in lifetime earnings.

That ratio, that's why we're arguing this is worth doing despite how much we hate it. Two and a half hours of the worst conversations we'll have in our professional lives versus half a million dollars or more over our careers. The math overwhelmingly favors having the conversations, even though our anxiety and our socialization and our past experiences tell us to avoid them at all costs. We can acknowledge all the reasons this feels impossible while still recognizing that the financial stakes are too high to let those feelings make the decision for us.

## Don't miss out!

Visit the website below and you can sign up to receive emails whenever Matthew Thomas publishes a new book. There's no charge and no obligation.

https://books2read.com/r/B-A-ICCIF-YDOCJ

BOOKS 2 READ

Connecting independent readers to independent writers.

Did you love *The Uncomfortable Conversation: Negotiation for People Who Hate Conflict*? Then you should read *Build and Sell Your First Online Course: Teach What You Know and Get Paid Doing It with the Proven Way to Turn Your Knowledge into Income*[1] by Ryan Papadopoulos!

[2]

**You don't need to be an expert. You just need a course people want.**

**Online Course (Even If You're Not an Expert)** is your no-hype, step-by-step guide to creating, launching, and selling your first (or next) online course — even if you're not famous, don't have a huge audience, or have no idea where to start.

This book is built for real people: freelancers, coaches, teachers, creators, and anyone with useful knowledge who wants to earn income online without gatekeeping, tech overwhelm, or trying to go viral on TikTok.

Inside, you'll learn how to pick a course topic people will actually pay for, even if you're not "the best" in your field. You'll get clear guidance on outlining your course, recording without stress, and building content fast — using what

1. https://books2read.com/u/mgpEqX

2. https://books2read.com/u/mgpEqX

you already know, in the format that works best for you (video, audio, PDF, slides, or hybrid).

You'll also learn how to price your course with confidence, choose the right platform (without wasting money on tech you don't need), and start selling — even with a small list or zero followers. We'll break down email strategy, pre-selling, launch sequences, and how to create an evergreen funnel that brings in sales while you sleep (no sketchy tactics).

Whether you're creating your first mini-course or want to scale a premium digital product, this book gives you the complete system to make it happen — even if you're introverted, low-energy, busy, or think the market's too crowded.

www.ingramcontent.com/pod-product-compliance
Lightning Source LLC
LaVergne TN
LVHW100326210926
848480LV00003B/1276